Better Together

BUILT TO LAST

THE BLUEPRINT FOR A RESILIENT MARRIAGE

By:

ERIC AND TACONDRA BROWN

Publishing in the United States of America

Publisher: Luminous Publishing
www.luminouspublishing.com
For bulk orders or other inquiries, email:
info@luminouspublishing.com

Table of Contents

The Enemy Can't Kill What God Anoints

Whether you are interested in getting married, engaged, or happily married you will discover that you are anointed to be a husband or wife to the individual God has for you. God will give you grace for your spouse. Don't take this grace for granted.

Introduction

What if the strength of your marriage isn't measured by how perfect it looks, but by how well it withstands life's battles and storms?

Marriage is often seen as a solid structure, built on love, trust, and commitment. But what happens when that foundation starts to crack? When life's challenges, unexpected detours, and hard seasons start eroding what once felt unshakable? The truth is, marriage is a beautiful journey, but let's be honest, it's not always easy. Every couple faces challenges: the daily grind of responsibilities, communication breakdowns, unmet expectations, and the natural ups and downs of life. Stress, financial pressures, parenting demands, and unresolved personal baggage can quietly chip away at even the strongest relationships.

For military marriages, those struggles are often magnified. Long deployments, frequent relocations, emotional strain, and the weight of sacrifice test a marriage in ways most people never experience. As an Army veteran who served 17 years with my wife by my side, we know all too well the problems, pressures, and pains that come with the privileges and purpose of the military life. Our marriage has faced more than its fair share of storms, some we saw coming, others that caught us completely off guard. Navigating both the military and civilian life, we often found ourselves wrestling with distance, not just the miles between us, but the emotional gap that can quietly grow over time. There were times when we felt like we were living separate lives instead of sharing one. The weight of service, stress from long separations, and the pressure to "stay strong" nearly pulled us apart.

Love got us started, but it wasn't enough to keep us going. It took intentional work, unwavering commitment, and God's grace to rebuild what life's storms tried to tear down. We don't share this to spotlight our struggles, but to offer hope: **if we can come back from the brink, so can you.** This book isn't just for military marriages, but we've been intentional about addressing the unique challenges military couples face while also honoring the battles that all marriages encounter. This book is our blueprint; built from lessons learned the hard way, designed to help you do more than survive marriage. It's here to help you build a relationship that's **better together and truly built to last.**

Our story didn't start with a fairy-tale romance. It all started with an awkward first kiss, surrounded by a few young friends and family in her brother's room after a waterpark birthday party when Tacondra was just nine years old. I was a lanky kid with glasses—*definitely not the picture of confidence.* And let's be honest, Tacondra wasn't exactly swooning over me. But that didn't stop me from acting like I had all the confidence in the world! Still, even back then, I knew there was something special between us. That day sparked a puppy love that would endure far more than we ever imagined—growing up together in church, navigating school, and facing challenges we never saw coming. What began as innocent affection blossomed into something deeper, but with that growth came the weight of life's realities. High school came with its fair share of relationship uncertainties, but nothing prepared us for the moment we found out Tacondra was pregnant. She was a senior in high school while I prepared for my new life as a soldier in the Army miles away. Suddenly, our worlds were turned upside down. What followed nine months later was a battle, both literal and emotional. At the time, Tacondra was still living in our home state of Florida when she went into labor at midnight. I was on the road, driving down from New York, desperately trying to make it in time, but I didn't. I missed the moment our daughter entered the world. And to be honest, things between Tacondra and me were far from ideal at the time. I experienced those two weeks with them as if they were only two minutes, and then, two months later, I deployed to war.

While I was navigating the realities of war, we were also trying to figure out how to be young parents and partners, because marriage wasn't yet on the table. Over a year later when I finally made the decision to pop the question, the proposal was anything but traditional. (*Nothing says young romance like a ring mailed from across the world*). And our first wedding? A quiet ceremony in upstate New York, far from family, in a small church with strangers that were just finishing up choir rehearsal. Tacondra's dad literally gave her away that day by phone! Yeah, we know—far from normal. But stories like this happen in the military life. (Thank goodness we were able to redeem that moment for him and our families years later). But at that time in our young hearts, we believed we were laying the foundation for a strong marriage. **Or so we thought.**

As the years passed, we realized that saying "I do" was just the beginning. The real challenge was learning how to stay married. Military life brought its own struggles, but even outside of that, we had to face the reality that love (and a baby together) alone wasn't enough. The cracks in our foundation weren't just from the deployments and distance that came with the military lifestyle, they came from within, from unspoken expectations, past wounds from childhood, and two young people still figuring out how to do life together.

Maybe our story doesn't mirror yours exactly, but if you've ever felt the weight of trying to hold it all together, if you've ever wondered whether your marriage can withstand the demands of life, or if you're committed to strengthening what you've already built, then this book is for you. We're not marriage counselors, and we don't claim to have a perfect formula. But with over 30 years of experience, through both the trenches and the triumphs of love and commitment, we've learned what it takes to fight for a marriage that lasts. This book isn't just a collection of stories from our journey; it's a practical guide filled with reflection questions, insights, and actionable steps for newlyweds, military couples, those in crisis, and those seeking to strengthen or rebuild their marriage.

Throughout these chapters, we'll share the lessons we've learned, the mistakes we've made, and the principles that kept us standing resilient when walking away seemed easier. Because our faith anchored our marriage, we rooted this book in scriptural wisdom and biblical principles. Whether you're a Believer or not, we believe the truths in these pages will resonate with your marriage and offer guidance, encouragement, and hope as you build something strong and lasting together. **Marriage isn't just a commitment—it's a battlefield.** And for those of us who believe in God's design for marriage, we know the attacks are not just random struggles; they're targeted assaults on a covenant meant to reflect Christ's love for the Church. But just like in any battle, victory is possible with the right strategy, the right mindset, and the right support.

So, if you're ready to build a marriage the best way, fight to rebuild what's been broken, or to create something even stronger than before, then let's get to work— **Together!**

PHASE 1: LAYING THE FOUNDATION

WITHOUT A SOLID BASE, IT'S BOUND TO SINK

Counting The Cost: Preparing For the Work of Marriage

Everything in life comes with a cost. Whether it's time, energy, money, or emotional investment. Nothing truly valuable is free. Marriage? No exception. It demands commitment, sacrifice, and intentional effort to build something lasting. But here's the kicker, most of us don't fully realize just how much it costs until we're already in it. When we got married, we were young and in love (well... *more like lust*), completely clueless about what we were stepping into. Like many couples who marry young, we assumed love alone would be enough to carry us through. It wasn't. Turns out, love isn't just warm feelings and butterflies all the time, it's a daily choice to show up, invest, and build, even when things get tough. In fact, Luke 14:28-30 gives us some solid advice:

"But don't begin until you count the cost. For who would begin construction of a building without first calculating the cost to see if there is enough money to finish it? Otherwise, you might complete only the foundation before running out of money, and then everyone would laugh at you. They would say, "There's the person who started that building and couldn't afford to finish it!"

Translation? Think it through before you commit. How many times have you jumped into something—whether a project, job, or relationship—only to realize halfway in that you weren't fully prepared? Or didn't want it after all? Marriage is no different. Many couples, especially young newlyweds entering the military, don't fully grasp what marriage entails. And let's be honest, unless you've had wise mentors or witnessed a healthy marriage firsthand, it's easy to get swept up in the fairy-tale version of love movies, social media, and well-meaning advice that sells the idea of marriage. But here's the truth: Marriage isn't just about love and good intentions. If we could hop in a time machine and give our younger selves one golden nugget of wisdom, it would be this: *Before you say, "I do," ask the right questions.*

Do you have mommy and daddy issues? *If so, let's heal that.*

Are there generational family patterns we need to break? *If so, what are they because we might not have the capacity for what comes with being married to one another.*

- What are your strengths and weaknesses?

14

- Do you know yourself—your values, triggers, and likes? *I know me! Do you know you?*
- What expectations do you have for marriage?
- What are your thoughts about roles and responsibilities? Be*cause, uh… SHE doesn't fold clothes!*
- How do you handle money? *Both of us can't be horrible spenders and broke!*
- What do you want in a lifelong partner, and are you willing to put in the work?

These aren't just deep questions, they're essential ones. *Literally, who's going to fold the laundry?* Unfortunately, we didn't go into marriage with this level of awareness. And it cost us. Time. Trust. Money. Prayers to baby Jesus. Years of trial, error, and figuring things out the hard way. If you're reading this thinking, *"Yep, I didn't count the cost either,"* breathe. Seriously. There's no shame here. The good news? It's never too late to reassess, unlearn toxic ways and patterns, and strengthen your relationship. Some folks think it's easier to throw in the towel than to fix what's broken. And while that might seem like the simpler route, lasting love requires effort. Of course, in some instances it's probably safer to throw in the towel and walk away. But this book isn't about that.

For us, divorce wasn't on the table, even though Tacondra may or may not have *tried* to run away a few times. (No judgment... relationships are *real* like that.) There were plenty of times we had to keep asking ourselves: *Is this worth holding on to? What are we willing to sacrifice to make this work? Are we committed to the effort it takes?*

So, whether you're married, engaged, or just thinking about taking that step, have you counted the cost? Have you truly considered what it means to build a life with someone? Relationships will stretch you. They require patience, communication, and a level of effort you might think you have but really don't. Your expectations of marriage, whether shaped by family, culture, or personal experiences, can lead to either fulfillment or frustration. Before marriage, it's easy to focus on the dreamy parts—the wedding, the honeymoon, the Pinterest-perfect "happily ever after." *Clearly, that wasn't our case in the beginning.* But real marriage? That's what starts when the cake's gone, the guests leave, and life shows up with bills, disagreements, and unexpected curveballs. For us, reality hit fast. Becoming parents unexpectedly as teens (*yeah...*we *weren't ready for that*) and navigating military life with long separations tested us in ways we couldn't have imagined. We quickly learned that love alone isn't enough. Building trust, letting go of unrealistic expectations, forgiving, and learning to communicate are non-negotiables. And let's be clear, *counting the cost* isn't a one-time deal. As you grow and life changes, you'll keep revisiting it.

If you're realizing you may not have fully prepared for the journey of marriage, don't panic. What matters is your *willingness* to do the work. Adjusting expectations and breaking unhealthy cycles isn't always easy. But the payoff? A marriage that's strong, fulfilling, and built to last. In the chapters ahead, we'll share the real struggles, lessons learned, and practical steps you can take to build (or rebuild) your marriage. Because here's the thing: resilient marriages aren't found, they're *built*. And anything worth building? It's worth *counting the cost.*

You wouldn't build a house without a blueprint, right? So why build a marriage without a plan? I mean, let's be honest! How many couples think about that...a blueprint for marriage? Especially when love is burning hot, or life throws those *oops moments* your way! But without a solid foundation and clear structure, things can quickly shatter under life's strain. Believe us, we've learned the hard way! So, how do you *intentionally* build a marriage that can weather the storms and stand the test of time? That's where *The Marriage Blueprint* comes in.

The Marriage Blueprint:

ARE YOU BUILDING WITH PURPOSE, OR JUST HOPING IT HOLDS

Every builder begins with the end in mind. Before the first brick is laid or a single nail is hammered, they start with a plan. A detailed blueprint that turns vision into reality. It's like an invisible dream on paper, mapping out every detail so the builder knows how to gather materials, count the cost, and get to work. You're probably still wondering: *Is there really such a thing as a marriage blueprint? And if so, what does that even look like?*

When we got married, we didn't have one. Honestly, we were winging it—armed with love, a baby, prayer, and a whole lot of optimism! Back then, there wasn't a flood of podcasts, YouTube channels, or detailed guides telling you how to "do marriage the right way." Nowadays? Couples are having deep conversations before saying *"I do"*. Discussing values, traditions, finances, careers, and yes, even whether one of them is secretly plotting to name their firstborn after their childhood pet. **(Spoiler: *Bear* is fitting for a puppy, not really for a kid.)**

They're mapping out their future, making sure they're on the same page. Some even invest time in premarital counseling to tackle potential landmines *before* they turn into "Why do you chew so loud?" arguments. Then there are people like us. You know the people—the ones who dive in headfirst with no plan, just romance, dreams, and maybe a surprise baby on the way. (*Sound familiar?*) They're fueled by passion and the belief that *"love will be enough." Real talk:* **Love is incredible, but it won't fix a broken AC in the middle of summer, settle a debate over who forgot to pay the light bill, or make your in-laws' "quick visit" shorter.** For that? You need communication, teamwork, and a solid budget!

If you didn't start your marriage with a blueprint, you're not alone! There are many couples out here in the world stumbling through with faith, love, and a whole lot of trial and error. And here's what we've learned: **there is no *one-size-fits-all* marriage blueprint.** We know what you're thinking: "Wait, wasn't the marriage blueprint the whole point of this book?" Yeah, you're right! But think about driving through a neighborhood of cookie-cutter houses…they might look the same from the outside, but inside? Completely different stories.

Marriage is not a cookie-cutter project. So, there is no cookie-cutter blueprint. Your relationship has its own unique design, built around your personalities, strengths, quirks, struggles, and shared dreams. Now do you know the funny thing about blueprints? They look perfect on paper…no cracks, no surprises. But the moment you start building, *life happens.* The foundation settles, unexpected challenges pop up, and you realize even the best plans need adjustments.

So, whether you started with a blueprint or you're figuring it out as you go, here's the key: **commit to building something strong and better than what you may have come from, together.** Adjust when life throws you lemons. Reinforce the areas that need extra care. Because at the end of the day, it's not about having a perfect blueprint. It's about building a marriage that lasts. One with a foundation that holds steady, not one that sinks when the storms come.

WHAT IS YOUR MARRIAGE BUILT ON

"For no one can lay a foundation other than that which is laid, which is Jesus Christ." - **1 Corinthians 3:11**

Back in our late twenties, we made the exciting decision to build our first home together. There was something thrilling about the process—finding a realtor, securing a home loan, and choosing a builder. But as exciting as it was, the journey quickly taught us that building a house is not for the faint of heart. What started as a dream soon met the reality of construction delays, decision fatigue, and the kind of stress that makes you question if granite countertops are really that important.

It all began around March 2012 when we pulled up to a barren hill in Copperas Cove, TX. A plot of land covered in dirt, rocks, and debris. It didn't look like much, just an open space holding the promise of what could be. We stood there imagining the walls that would soon rise, the rooms we'd fill with laughter (and let's be honest, a few heated debates), and the memories waiting to be made. But as the process unfolded, one truth became crystal clear: **no** matter how beautiful the design, the foundation had to be solid. Fancy finishes and curb appeal meant nothing if the ground beneath wasn't stable. Two important lessons emerged from the start of our home-building journey:

The soil had to be stable enough to hold the foundation. The foundation had to be strong enough to bear the weight of what we were building.

Looking back, it's hard to miss the parallel between building a house and building a marriage.

The Soil of Marriage

Think about it. What good is a stunning house if it's built on sinking ground? The same goes for relationships. You can have all the outward signs of a perfect marriage—cute date nights, Instagram-worthy vacations, and matching Christmas pajamas—but if the underlying ground is unstable, cracks will show when life gets heavy.

So, *what kind of soil is your marriage built on?*

Is it rooted in trust, open communication, and emotional safety? Or are there unresolved issues beneath the surface (old wounds, hidden fears, lingering insecurities) that could weaken your foundation over time? We get it. When we first got married, we thought love would be enough to carry us through any trial! And while love *is* essential, love without understanding, intentionality, and preparation is like planting seeds in rocky soil; it may sprout fast, but it won't survive when storms roll in.

Jesus' Parable of the Sower in **Mark 4:1-9** paints this picture beautifully. Seeds scattered on different types of soil yield very different results. Some are eaten by birds, others wither on rocky ground, and some are choked by thorns. But the seed that falls on *good soil*? It thrives, producing a rich and lasting harvest. In marriage, seeds represent things like love, trust, communication, commitment, respect, intimacy, and personal growth. But before planting those seeds, you've got to check the condition of the soil...your heart and your partner's heart.

Ask yourself:

- Is my heart ready to carry the weight of lifelong commitment?
- Have I dealt with past wounds, childhood hurts, and adult insecurities that might sabotage our growth?
- Am I sowing seeds that nurture a thriving marriage, or am I letting unresolved issues choke out our potential?

Just like builders' clear debris before laying a foundation, you must clear out anything that could compromise the strength of your relationship. That means addressing baggage you've been lugging around, healing from past heartbreaks, and establishing transparency and trust from the get-go. *Real talk*: No one builds a house expecting it to collapse. Yet, how many marriages fall apart because the groundwork was never solid? Building a marriage requires more than romantic dates and sex; it demands preparing the ground, building a strong foundation, and constructing a structure that can withstand life's inevitable storms.

So, again we ask: *What is your marriage built on?* Because a beautiful exterior means nothing if what's underneath can't hold it up.

Foundation Depth

The strength of a foundation must match the weight of what's being built.

Imagine trying to build a skyscraper on a foundation meant for a doghouse. No matter how stunning the design, the structure won't hold. Marriage works the same way. If you want a strong, lasting, purpose-driven union, you need a foundation deep enough to support it.

Before any house is built, the land is surveyed, the soil tested, and the foundation laid with care. In many ways, dating is that phase where you get to know each other's values, beliefs, character, and emotional stability. It's about making sure what you're building can withstand the pressures that life inevitably brings. There's no universal timeline for how long this phase should last. What matters is the depth of understanding you build during it.

We didn't fully grasp that at first. "Love" at any age, but especially a young age, has a funny way of clouding judgment. The excitement of being in a relationship can make it easy to rush into marriage (and more) without pausing to consider what you're building on. We learned (the hard way) that love alone couldn't fill the cracks in our foundation. It took intentional growth, self-awareness, and a commitment to keep strengthening our relationship—something that first began when we were kids, playing the piano and drums together as a team in church.

And if you're a Believer? The deepest, strongest foundation you can build on is **Jesus Christ**—the Chief Cornerstone. Scripture reminds us:

"The stone that the builders rejected has become the cornerstone." - Psalm 118:22

In ancient architecture, the cornerstone was the first stone laid, the reference point for every other stone. If it was off, the entire structure would be unstable. The same is true in marriage: If Christ isn't the cornerstone, everything else can fall out of alignment. Without His guidance and presence at the center, relationships can fall apart under pressure...whether from life's demands, cultural expectations, or personal struggles.

IF YOU'RE A BELIEVER, ASK YOURSELF:

- Is your marriage aligned with God's design?
- Is Christ truly the foundation, or just a decorative piece?
- Are you building on His principles, or constructing something based on personal desires and societal norms?

If you've reflected on those questions and realized that your marriage may not fully align with God's design, don't be discouraged. Ours wasn't completely aligned either. Awareness is the first step toward transformation. Just like building a house, you can't establish a strong structure without first preparing the ground. Even if Christ is the foundation, the soil of your hearts must be ready to receive and support what you're building together. A firm foundation isn't just about spiritual alignment; it requires intentional inner work to clear out anything that could cause cracks down the road. That's where the real work begins…laying the groundwork.

LAYING THE GROUNDWORK

Building something that lasts requires digging deep before you build high. In marriage, that digging is the inner work, unpacking personal baggage, healing old wounds, and cultivating transparency and trust. The effort you put in at this stage will determine the strength and longevity of your relationship. No marriage is perfect, but couples who take time to lay a solid foundation are the ones best equipped to weather life's storms.

Looking back, we didn't realize how rocky our soil was until years into our marriage. Sure, we grew up together and had history as a foundation. Yes, we planted seeds of love, but unspoken resentment, past hurts, guilt, and unhealed wounds cluttered the soil of our hearts. Love tried to grow, but the roots struggled to dig deep. It wasn't until well into our journey (over a decade in) that we truly grasped how our unresolved issues were undermining the foundation of our relationship.

Unpacking Personal Baggage

Let's take a moment to address the rocky seed-chokers of marriage, those hidden things that quietly stunt growth. We all bring a suitcase into our relationships, packed with history, beliefs, and life experiences. Some of what we carry is valuable, like lessons learned and resilience gained. But other things? They're emotional clutter: unresolved wounds, fears, insecurities, and habits that don't serve us or our spouse. Left unchecked, this personal baggage doesn't just sit quietly in a corner. It shows up, often when you least expect it, in misunderstandings, conflicts, and unmet expectations.

Unpacking that baggage isn't about having everything figured out before you say, "I do." It's about awareness, recognizing what you're carrying so you can lighten the load and avoid weighing down your relationship. Many of us walk into marriage with two heavy bags: **past wounds** and **picture-perfect expectations.** Movies, fairy tales, and social media often sell the idea of marriage as a never-ending honeymoon.

But real life? It's dishes, deadlines, disagreements, and choosing to love even on the days you don't feel like it.

Take a moment to reflect:

- What did I learn about love and relationships growing up?
- How have past friendships, family dynamics, or romantic relationships shaped my view of commitment?
- What fears or insecurities am I bringing into this relationship?

Some of us grew up witnessing broken or toxic relationships, creating fears of repeating the same patterns. Others absorbed romanticized ideals that fall apart under the weight of real life. Healing from these misconceptions isn't a onetime fix, it's an ongoing process that requires intentionality and grace.

So, what does that process look like?

- **Recognizing unhealthy patterns:** Notice where your habits or reactions stem from. Is it past hurt? Fear? Old defense mechanisms?

- **Replace fear-based thinking with truth:** Not every disagreement spells disaster, and no spouse is perfect (*newsflash: neither are you*). Growth happens when we stop making every flaw a deal-breaker.
- **Seek growth:** Counseling, mentorship, self-reflection, and honest conversations with your spouse aren't just options, they're investments in your relationship's future.

One of the biggest myths about marriage is that *love alone is enough.* Love is powerful, but without emotional maturity, intentional effort, and a willingness to grow, love can wither under pressure. Healing your past, whether before marriage or during it, creates a stronger, healthier foundation for your future together.

GENDER ROLES: WHO'S SUPPOSED TO DO WHAT!

Let's go ahead and throw this topic in quickly before moving into the *deeper* stuff. One of the quickest ways to set yourself up for frustration in marriage is to assume your spouse *just knows* what they're supposed to do. *They don't.* And honestly? Chances are, you don't either. When we first got married, we thought we had it figured out. Roles? Easy! Or so we assumed—without *ever* actually talking about them. We just believed the other person would magically do things or pick up where we left off. *That didn't happen.* Cue the classic *"I thought you were going to do that!"* arguments. Sound familiar?

Let's be real: Did you and your spouse ever sit down and officially assign who handles what?

- Who's doing the dishes?
- Paying the bills?
- Taking out the trash?
- Cooking dinner?
- FOLDING THE LAUNDRY?! (*It's me...Tacondra. I hate folding laundry. Unless, of course, it's warm towels!*).

Didn't have this discussion? Yeah... us neither. And kudos to you if you did! Like most couples, we just did what we knew, usually based on what we saw growing up. The problem? What worked (or didn't work) in our childhood homes didn't always translate into *our* marriage. *(Lucky for her, I enjoy folding laundry because it was something I did with my mom and grandma growing up-***Eric.***)*

Society loves to hand out neat little packages labeled "husband does this" and "wife does that," complete with the promise of a happily ever after. ***Lies.*** If you've been married longer than 24 hours, you already know there's no universal manual for this. Your marriage isn't your parents' marriage or that picture-perfect couple you see on Facebook. Maybe your husband enjoys cooking while you'd rather manage the finances. Maybe yard work isn't his thing, but you secretly love mowing the lawn (*hello, free workout!*). Maybe *neither* of you are great at cleaning, and hiring a housekeeper saves your sanity! (*No shame—wish we could've afforded that early on in our marriage!*)

Here's the truth: Marriage is a team sport, not a job description.

Instead of forcing traditional roles to fit, figure out what works *for **you***. Instead of waiting for resentment to build over that pile of dishes, just talk about it. Seriously, have the conversation. Be honest about what you dislike (because let's face it...no one's lining up to scrub the toilet).

Here are some simple ways to *make roles work*:

- **Divide and Conquer:** Play to your strengths. If you're a budgeting pro and your spouse is a meal-prep ninja, roll with it.

- **Be Flexible:** Just because you start with certain roles doesn't mean they're set in stone. Life changes, adjust accordingly.

- **Check In Regularly:** Don't wait until both of you are silently fuming over unwashed laundry. Quick "team huddles" help keep things fair.

- **Remember You're on the Same Team:** This isn't about keeping score. It's about building a life together—without passive-aggressive sticky notes about whose turn it is to clean the bathroom.

At the end of the day, gender roles in marriage aren't about sticking to traditions or meeting societal expectations, they're about **partnership, teamwork, and**

saving both of you from losing your minds. So, talk it out, figure out what works, and, most importantly, laugh when things go hilariously wrong. *Because trust us, they will.*

Shining a light on these hidden struggles won't solve everything overnight. But the more you unpack before laying the first brick of your life together, the less unnecessary stress you'll drag into your future.

TRANSPARENCY AND TRUST AS THE FIRST STEPS TO A SOLID FOUNDATION

A house can't stand on a shaky foundation, and neither can a marriage. Transparency and trust are the cornerstones that keep a relationship steady, even when storms hit. The beautiful thing about our story is that we developed a friendship in our youth. But let's be real, trust wasn't exactly our strong suit. In fact, we barely knew how to spell trust, let alone build it! Transparency means being real; no masks, no half-truths.

It's about:
- Sharing your past honestly, without fear of rejection.
- Voicing your expectations, fears, and dreams.
- Addressing conflict head-on instead of sweeping it under the rug.

And trust? That's built brick by brick. It's showing up consistently by keeping your word and creating a safe space where vulnerability isn't punished but embraced. Without transparency, resentment can sneak in through the cracks. Without trust, doubts and insecurities chip away at the bond you're trying to build. A relationship held together by secrets and avoidance may look fine on the outside, but under pressure, it collapses. When transparency and trust are your first building blocks, you lay a foundation strong enough to withstand challenges, deepen intimacy, and grow stronger with time. So, start by unpacking, healing, and building with honesty and intention because what you build today shapes the legacy you leave tomorrow.

MARRIAGE: A LIFELONG CONSTRUCTION PROJECT

Marriage isn't a *one-and-done* event. It's an ongoing project. Even with the strongest foundation, every structure needs regular maintenance, repairs, and occasional renovations. Life changes. People grow. Challenges arise. But when your foundation is firm, rooted in truth, love, and resilience, your relationship can withstand the toughest storms. Wherever you are on your journey, engaged, newly married, or decades in, your marriage deserves a foundation that can stand the test of time.

Take a moment to pause and evaluate:

- Is the soil of your relationship healthy and ready for growth?
- Is your foundation deep enough for what you're building?
- And most importantly, if you're a Believer, is Christ your cornerstone?

We recognize not everyone reading this may share our faith. If Jesus isn't your foundation, then who or what is guiding your relationship? Who's your model, your mentor, your motivation for building something that lasts? And if these questions stir your conviction, don't be discouraged. Consider it an invitation to realign and rebuild. The good news? **God is the Master Builder, and He specializes in restoration.** No matter how shaky your foundation feels today, there's hope. With intentional effort, honest conversations, counseling, prayer, and a willingness to grow, you *can* strengthen your marriage. The strongest marriages aren't the ones that never face struggles. They're the ones that stand firm because they were built (or rebuilt) on the *right* foundation. And it's never too late to start building better.

We're about to dig a little deeper into the foundation of marriage, especially when it comes to the **spiritual side** and what a **Godly marriage** looks like. Now, if the talk of God and spiritual matters isn't really your thing, don't worry. We're not here to preach at you. We promise to keep it real (and maybe even crack a joke or two along the way). But if you're not quite ready for this kind of meat, you've got options: **skip ahead** or **chew on what resonates and spit out what doesn't.** Either way, we invite you to stick around. You might just discover some nourishing truth in the mix.

Covenant vs. Contract

When it comes to marriage, how do you view it? Is it just a legal contract…a piece of paper binding two people under the law? Or is it something deeper? Sure, marriage comes with paperwork, joint accounts, and sharing the last slice of pizza (which, let's be honest, is a big deal). But God designed marriage to be more than a legal agreement. It's a covenant. A sacred, lifelong commitment between a husband, a wife, and God Himself. Fun fact: the first marriage (hello, Adam and Eve) didn't come with paperwork. Honestly, if Adam had needed a prenup, we might not even be here! So, what's the difference between a contract and a covenant? Trust us—it matters.

WHAT'S A CONTRACT

A **contract** is a legally binding agreement where both parties agree to terms, usually involving an exchange of services, money, or goods. If one person fails to hold up their end of the deal, legal action can follow. Think of it like your phone plan: miss enough payments, and your service gets cut off. Simple. But here's the thing, marriage is *not* a business deal (or at least, it shouldn't be).

Contracts are **conditional**:

- *"I'll do this if you do that."*
- *"If you meet my expectations, I'll stay committed."*

Unfortunately, this mentality sneaks into some marriages, especially in settings like the military, where some people tie the knot for housing allowances or financial benefits. While it might seem convenient, contract marriages built on benefits rather than covenant and commitment rarely end well. We've seen our share of military marriages fail because they were bonding together for bands, not for love that last. Marriage deserves a **higher**

standard than being used as a loophole for extra pay. We've also seen military marriages with the potential to thrive, but the unique challenges of the culture got the best of them, causing covenants to crumble under the pressure.

What's a Covenant

Now let's talk about covenant. A word that carries far more weight.

Webster's Dictionary defines a covenant as "a written agreement or promise under seal between two or more parties for the performance of some action." Sounds like a contract, right? But here's the key difference: a covenant isn't just about obligation, it's about devotion.

A covenant is unconditional:
- *"I'm committed to you, no matter what."*
- *"I'm here for the better and the worse—when life is easy and when it's messy."*

When you stand at the altar and say, *"for better or worse,"* God isn't just listening, He takes those words seriously. **Ecclesiastes 5:4** reminds us:

"When you make a vow to God, do not be late in paying it; for He takes no delight in fools. Pay what you vow!"

That's not just poetic wedding language; it's a reality check. **Vows carry *weight*.** They're not just for show or to impress your guests. They're a covenant before God, meant to hold strong through every season of life. Unlike a contract (which one can negotiate or dissolve), faith, love, and divine accountability seal a covenant. *BLOOD! Yep, this isn't your everyday handshake agreement.* Throughout Scripture, God models true covenant love: unwavering, sacrificial, and enduring. That's the level of commitment marriage requires, *not convenience. Commitment.*

COMMITMENT: MORE THAN JUST A GOOD IDEA

Commitment sounds noble, right? But let's be real...*sticking with something is easier said than done.* It's like signing up for a gym membership in January—exciting at first, but by February, you're just funding the place.

Commitment is more than a feel-good concept. It's the **daily choice** to show up even when you don't feel like it. Even when your spouse forgets to take out the trash (*again*). Even when you're navigating job stress, parenting struggles, or those *"why do you fold the clothes like that?"* debates.

Real commitment says:

- *"I choose you when things are good."*
- *"I choose you when things are hard."*
- *"I choose you—even when I don't feel like choosing you."*

And let's be honest, commitment can feel scary. Maybe you've committed to something (or someone) before and got burned. Maybe you experienced hurt, disappointment, or letdown. If that's you, it's okay to try again. Commitment isn't about perfection, it's about perseverance.

Ask yourself:
- *What am I truly committed to?*
- *Do I show the same dedication to my marriage as I do to my job, hobbies, or favorite Netflix series?*
- *Am I genuinely invested, or just going through the motions?*

Connection isn't the same as commitment. Just because you feel connected to someone doesn't mean you're committed. True commitment is about choosing to stay, even when it's hard. **Ephesians 5:25** (MSG) challenges husbands:

> *"Husbands, go all out in your love for your wives, exactly as Christ did for the church—a love marked by giving, not getting."*

Love and commitment go hand in hand. One without the other is incomplete. Think again about the things in your life that require real commitment. Whether it's your career, your personal growth, or your faith, each of them demands intention, effort, and consistency. The same is true for marriage. The person you commit to should not only be someone you love but someone who inspires you to grow, someone who sparks your purpose, and pushes you to become your best self. Shifting your mindset from me to we in marriage is another commitment often overlooked. When you marry, you and your spouse are no longer two separate individuals, you become one. Oneness is more than physical…it's emotional, spiritual, and mental. This is the foundation of biblical marriage:

"This is now bone of my bones and flesh of my flesh; she shall be called 'woman,' for she was taken out of man. That is why a man leaves his father and mother and is united to his wife, and they become one flesh." Genesis 2:23-24

Oneness in marriage requires a new mindset. This means letting go of self-centered thinking and embracing a shared life built on forgiveness, patience, and unconditional love. We're about to dive deeper into unity, but it isn't something that happens automatically, it's something you build, protect, and fight for daily. When you commit to keeping the bond of peace and choosing love, you create a marriage that is whole, fruitful, and a true reflection of God's design. At the end of the day, we want you to remember that commitment isn't just about staying, it's about choosing to stay, again and again.

VOWS REVISITED: A COVENANT, NOT JUST A CONTRACT

This is an **interactive experience** where you and your spouse can:

o   Revisit your vows together

o   Reflect on the scriptures

o   Have honest discussions about where you struggle

o   Reaffirm your commitment

Marriage Vows

"I, ___, take you, ___, for my lawful wife/husband, to have and to hold from this day forward, for better, for worse, for richer, for poorer, in sickness and health, until death do us part."

Let's go over these vows line upon line because what we have found in most cases of couples who marry young is that we only mean for better and rich-stay, for worse or poor-go! This certainly is not the case for all, but we have witnessed more than our fair share of young marriages end in divorce at the mercy of financial problems and worse circumstances.

"I _____" – A Personal Declaration

When you say your name, you are personally taking responsibility for the commitment you are about to make. No one else can make these vows on your behalf. It's a declaration that you, as an individual, are entering into this covenant with full awareness.

Scripture Reference: Ecclesiastes 5:4-5 – *"When you make a vow to God, do not delay in fulfilling it. He has no pleasure in fools; fulfill your vow."*

"Take You _____"– The Exclusive Bond

You aren't making this vow to just *anyone*, you are making it to one specific person. This means that no one else in your life should have the same level of emotional, spiritual, and physical intimacy as your spouse.

Scripture Reference: Numbers 30:2 "If a man makes a vow to the Lord or swears an oath to bind himself by some agreement, he shall not break his word; he shall do according to all that proceeds out of his mouth."

"To be my lawful wife/husband"
– The Covenant of Marriage

Marriage is not just a legal contract; it is a divine covenant. The laws of the land recognize marriage, but long before governments existed, God established marriage as a holy union.

Scripture Reference- Genesis 2:18 And the Lord God said, "*It is* not good that man should be alone; I will make him a helper comparable to him.

"To Have and to Hold"– Love, Responsibility, and Protection of Marriage

"To have" means to cherish, take responsibility for, and care for one another. It's not about ownership, it's about commitment.

"To hold" symbolizes protection, security, and comfort. It means that your spouse should find safety in your love, knowing you will stand beside them through everything.

Scripture Reference: Ephesians 5:33 "Each one of you also must love his wife as he loves himself, and the wife must respect her husband."

"From This Day Forward" – A Lifelong Commitment

This part of the vow is a prophetic declaration. It is a promise to commit, no matter what happens in the future. Love is not just about the past, it's a decision you make daily moving forward.

Scripture Reference: Philippians 3:13-14 –
"Forgetting what is behind and straining toward what is ahead,
I press on toward the goal to win the prize for which God has
called me heavenward in Christ Jesus."

"For Better"– Celebrating the Good Times

It's easy to love someone when life is smooth. This part of the vow is about being present and appreciative when things are good, when love is strong, and when life feels full of blessings. It also means I'll love the best parts of you always.

Scripture Reference: James 1:17 – *"Every good and perfect gift is from above, coming down from the Father of the heavenly lights, who does not change like shifting shadows."*

"For Worse"– Enduring Hardships Together

Marriage will test you. There will be moments of disappointment, pain, and struggle. This vow is about choosing to stay even when it's uncomfortable. None of us want the worst to happen in our marriage but it's inevitable and a marriage that can't be tested **can't be trusted**.

Scripture Reference: Romans 5:3-4 – *"We also glory in our sufferings, because we know that suffering produces perseverance; perseverance, character; and character, hope."*

"For Richer" – Stewarding Blessings Wisely

A financially stable season can be a **blessing or a curse** depending on how you handle it. Will prosperity bring you closer together or create division? For some this may be the only part of the vow they're concerned with because **who wants to be poor?**

Scripture Reference: Luke 16:10 – *"Whoever can be trusted with very little can also be trusted with much."*

"For Poorer"– Standing Strong in Lack

Money problems are one of the **top causes** of divorce. What happens when financial drought hits and seasons of stripping show up? This vow means **you are choosing love over material security**.

Scripture Reference: Philippians 4:12-13 – *"I know what it is to be in need, and I know what it is to have plenty. I have learned the secret of being content in any and every* *situation, whether well fed or hungry, whether living in plenty or in want. I can do all this through Him who gives me strength."*

"In Sickness and Health" – Loving Through Every Condition

This vow means that love isn't conditional on health, ability, or wellness. Whether it's a short-term illness or a lifelong condition, **you commit to being there for your spouse.**

Scripture Reference: Galatians 6:2 – *"Carry each other's burdens, and in this way, you will fulfill the law of Christ."*

"Until Death Do Us Part"– A Covenant for Life

The weightiest part of the vow…**this is for life.** This isn't a contract you can back out of when it gets tough; it is a sacred covenant that only ends when one of you takes your last breath. It's very hard to imagine life without your husband or wife, but this statement stamps the expiration date on the journey together.

Scripture Reference: Mark 10:9 – *"Therefore what God has joined together, let no one separate."*

Reflection Questions:

1. How do I currently view my marriage vows? Do I see them as a covenant before God or just a legal commitment?

2. What does "for better or for worse" truly mean to me? Have I been faithful to this vow in my actions and mindset?

3. How do I respond to financial struggles in marriage? Do I allow money to dictate the strength of my commitment?

4. Am I embracing my role as a husband/wife according to God's design, or am I influenced by personal expectations and cultural norms?

5. How can I actively "have and hold" my spouse in a way that nurtures our emotional, spiritual, and physical connection?

6. Have I invited God into my marriage daily, or do I only seek Him in difficult times?

7. What steps can I take to ensure that my marriage continues to grow in love, faith, and unity?

8. How do I handle sickness, hardship, or loss in my marriage? What fears do I need to surrender to God?

9. If I were to renew my vows today, what new understanding would I bring to them?

10. How can I encourage and uplift my spouse to be all that God has called them to be?

These reflections will help deepen the understanding of the commitment made in marriage and allow you to assess your journey with honesty and faith.

Covenants Are Worth Fighting For

Not all marriages are meant to be, let's be clear about that. But many with the potential to thrive fall apart because they operate like contracts: conditional, performance-based, and quick to dissolve under difficulty. When stress mounts, when expectations aren't met, when the road gets rocky, the enemy says: "You didn't sign up for this." *RUNNNNNN!!!" (Or just walk away...your choice).*

But here's the thing: the enemy isn't interested in breaking contracts; **he specializes in breaking covenants.** Why? Because covenants carry *power*. They create *legacies*. They shape *generations*. **And the greatest threat to any covenant is division.** A house divided can't stand, and the enemy knows it. That's why he sows seeds of miscommunication, resentment, unforgiveness, bitterness, and isolation. But when husband and wife stand united— spiritually, emotionally, and mentally—they become an unshakable force.

Now, unity doesn't mean you'll agree on everything (*you won't*). It means you're standing on the same team, fighting for —and not against— each other. Bottom line, marriage isn't just a contract with conditions, it's a **covenant** and lifelong commitment. It's not about convenience. It's about choosing to stay, choosing to fight, and choosing *each other in unity* every day. So, how do you cultivate true unity in marriage? Let's explore the foundation of oneness and the power it holds in strengthening your bond.

PHASE 2: FRAMING THE STRUCTURE

THE BONES OF A HOUSE DETERMINE ITS STRENGTH

The Power of Unity

The enemy knows something about marriage that many couples forget: **unity is powerful.** That's why unity in marriage is under constant attack. When two people stand together in harmony, they become a force that's not easily shaken. In the military, soldiers wear uniforms not just for practical purposes but as a symbol of identity and unity. It's easy to spot who's on your team when everyone wears the same colors, reinforcing the mission and belonging.

We noticed a similar effect when we hosted our *Built2Last Marriages* boot camp. Every couple wore their *Built2Last Marriages* T-shirt—an outward symbol of oneness, not just within their marriages but within a larger community fighting for the same goal: a stronger marriage.

Ever thought about the word uniform? Let's break down this word.

- **UNI = One**
- **FORM = Shape, Appearance, Structure**

In marriage, *unity* is about becoming one form—two individuals moving in sync, sharing a common vision, and forming a partnership that reflects a single purpose. Have you ever noticed how some couples literally begin to look alike the longer they're together? It's not a coincidence. But real talk: unity doesn't just happen. It's built, brick by brick, through intentional choices and sometimes, hard conversations.

THE TUG-OF-WAR OF MARRIAGE

In the early days of marriage, it's common for couples to feel like they're on opposite ends of a rope, pulling against each other's upbringing, beliefs, habits, and expectations. Arguments can spark over the simplest things: where to live, how to budget, whose family traditions to follow, or who's supposed to *fold the laundry*. Before long, marriage can feel like a relentless tug-of-war, with both spouses digging in rather than moving forward. But here's where everything shifts: **Stop fighting against your spouse and start fighting with them.**

When you choose *unity over division*, you:
- Release unnecessary tension
- Strengthen your bond
- Move toward each other and toward God.

We learned quickly that **marriage is a test of *selflessness*, not selfishness.** As long as you're pulling in opposite directions against one another, progress is impossible. But when you align as one, your marriage gains the resilience to withstand any storm.

THE POWER OF MEETING IN MARRIAGE

God's presence thrives in an atmosphere of peace and unity, not in environments filled with constant strife and contention. Yet, too often, couples let unresolved conflict drive a wedge between them.

Amos 3:3 asks,

> *"Can two walk together, except they be agreed?"*

Many interpret this verse as needing to *agree* on *everything,* but we have revelation of a difference. Unity isn't just about thinking the same way, it's about **coming together** with the same purpose of going somewhere. Even with differing dinner plans, you and your spouse can still be deeply unified in your goals, values, and commitment. But that only happens when you have made it a point **to meet** and discuss these types of things.

Think about how everyday meetings work. If you've got a health concern, you don't barge into a doctor's office demanding immediate treatment—you **schedule an appointment**. The same principle applies to marriage. If you don't make time to meet, you'll struggle to walk in unity. ***Pro Tip:*** *Schedule regular check-ins. Talk about your dreams, plans, and even the small stuff. Silence creates space for assumptions, and assumptions breed division.*

Anyway, the same principle applies in every area of life; whether interviewing for a job, catching up with friends over coffee, or setting aside time for personal prayer. Even God keeps His appointments with us, but the question is, *do we keep ours? (Hello!)*

Here are some practical ways to build stronger unity by connecting with your spouse:

Meet to Discuss Direction: Your spouse can't help you reach your destination if they don't know where you're headed. Regularly share your goals and vision for the future.

Husbands, Share Your Vision: Discuss with your wife what she can do to help meet the vision you have for your family. And if you don't have one, lean into the voice of your wife. She just might be the stronger visionary between the two of you. Lead with clarity. When both spouses understand and align with the family's direction, navigating challenges becomes smoother.

Meet About Agreements *and* Disagreements: It's easy to agree on fun stuff like vacation plans, buying fancy cars, or deciding what to eat! But what about the tough topics that often go unaddressed: paying bills, money management, parenting styles, submission, in-law dynamics? Oh, and what to eat, again! Don't avoid hard conversations. Facing them head-on fosters trust and unity.

Remember, you're a Team: The goal isn't to *win* arguments but to *win* together.

Disagreements are inevitable, but they don't have to be destructive. How you handle them determines whether they weaken or strengthen your bond. Paul's words in Ephesians 4:3 is clear:

"Make every effort to keep the unity of the Spirit through the bond of peace, [each individual working together to make the whole successful.]"

Your goal should always be to navigate conflicts with wisdom and grace, making every effort to protect the unity and peace within your relationship. We'd be lying if we said this process of becoming one is easy. *It isn't.* Unity takes effort. Peace is intentional. And Love is the glue that binds them together. God **is** love, and love is the force that binds a marriage together in perfect harmony. When a husband and wife dwell in unity, they create an atmosphere where God's presence can abide. Scripture tells us that **perfect unity is where God dwells.** In biblical terms, "perfect" unity doesn't mean *flawless;* it means *mature.* Mature love can handle disagreements without division.

Mature love means being:
- Clothed in compassion and kindness (Colossians 3:12-15)
- Quick to forgive and slow to anger
- Choosing love over pride

The more intentional you are about meeting, talking, and aligning your hearts in unity, the stronger your bond will be. Remember: unity in marriage doesn't happen by chance, it is cultivated through intentional choices and a commitment to love as Christ loves. Here are **four essential keys** that will help strengthen the bond between you and your spouse:

Four Keys to Building Unity in Marriage

1. Humility

Valuing Your Spouse Above Yourself: True humility is not about thinking less of yourself, but about **thinking of yourself less** and prioritizing your spouse's needs. Scripture teaches:

"Do nothing from selfishness or empty conceit [through factional motives or strife], but with [an attitude of] humility [being neither arrogant nor self-righteous], regard others as more important than yourselves."
Philippians 2:3 (AMP)

Humility requires stepping out of the spotlight and allowing your spouse to shine. Humility isn't self-degradation, it's prioritizing your spouse's needs without losing yourself. However, this can be difficult if past wounds, broken trust, or fears of intimacy have created barriers. **Pride, self-entitlement, and unhealed hurts** can hinder unity in marriage, making it vital to surrender those struggles and embrace a posture of selflessness.

2. Gentleness: Choosing Kindness Over Harshness

Gentleness is often mistaken for weakness, but it is strength under control. It is the choice to handle your spouse with care, patience, and understanding rather than responding with aggression or frustration. Paul instructs husbands specifically in this area:

"Husbands, dwell with your wife in an understanding way..."
- 1 Peter 3:7

"Husbands, love your wives and do not be harsh with them."
- Colossians 3:19

In moments of tension, our natural tendency is to **react** instead of **respond**, to defend ourselves rather than to seek understanding. But when we choose gentleness, we create a safe space for honest communication and emotional connection. Gentleness creates a safe space where vulnerability can thrive.

3. Patience: Enduring with Grace

Patience isn't passive, it's actively choosing to extend grace when challenges arise in marriage and choosing to remain calm and loving when growth feels slow.

"Be completely humble and gentle; be patient, bearing with one another in love." **Ephesians 4:2**

Patience isn't something we are born with; it is a muscle that's developed over time. A marriage built on patience will withstand storms, setbacks, and seasons of struggle.

4. Love: The Foundation of Unity

Love isn't just a feeling, it's an **intentional choice, a daily action, and a lifelong commitment.** Without love, unity cannot exist. Christ demonstrated the **ultimate love** by sacrificing Himself for us, and in marriage, we are called to reflect that same selfless, sacrificial love.

"Husbands, love your wives, just as Christ loved the church and gave himself up for her."

— **Ephesians 5:25**

"Love is patient, love is kind. It does not envy, it does not boast, it is not proud." — **1 Corinthians 13:4**

To **love well** in marriage means to:

- Choose kindness even when you feel frustrated.
- Extend forgiveness instead of holding onto resentment.
- Prioritize connection over being right.
- Serve your spouse without expecting something in return.

You might have noticed some points we've shared sound a bit repetitive…that's intentional. Certain truths are worth repeating, especially when it comes to fighting together, not against each other. We cannot stress this principle enough. So, let's dig a little deeper into what that really looks like in marriage.

FIGHTING TOGETHER, NOT AGAINST EACH OTHER

In the military, you learn one fundamental truth that stands above the rest: **you never go into battle alone.** Your battle buddy is there to protect you, cover your blind spots, and stand beside you in the fight—not against you. Marriage operates the same way. Yet too often life's demands can make spouses fall into the trap of seeing each other as enemies rather than allies, turning your marriage into a battlefield where you fight against each other instead of fighting for each other. It's important to **recognize the true enemy in marriage.**

From the Garden of Eden to today, the enemy's strategy hasn't changed—he isolates, sows doubt and exploits communication breakdowns. Think about all the small, petty arguments that you and your spouse seem to have repeatedly. The disagreements about responsibilities, the mistakes that feel like they push you further apart...these are not random. The enemy thrives on confusion, whispering lies into our hearts, twisting words, and magnifying offenses so that we become **so focused on**

the battle against each other that we fail to see the battle we should be fighting together.

My wife always tells me, *"If you don't talk to me, the enemy will."* That statement alone reveals the importance of **constant, open, and honest communication in marriage.** In our Built2Last Marriage boot camp, we had one spouse blindfold the other and guide them verbally through a minefield of obstacles. It was hilarious to watch, but also incredibly revealing. Some couples did great at communicating clearly, while others struggled with frustration, misunderstandings, and lack of trust. This exercise perfectly demonstrated how navigating life together requires constant trust, guidance, and communication. Because without it, you're blindly walking through a battlefield, and the enemy is waiting for you to misstep so he can **divide and conquer.** The enemy knows that a couple fighting each other makes his job easier as they are already doing the hard work of destruction for him. Every argument, every misunderstanding, and every moment of silence between you and your spouse can either be a weapon in the enemy's hands or an opportunity for you both to fight together. The question is: *Who are you fighting?* Remember this, **your spouse is not your competition.** They are your co-laborer, your teammate, your **battle buddy.**

FIGHTING HAND-IN-HAND, NOT HAND-TO-HAND

The military trains us in hand-to-hand combat, a fighting technique used when engaging with an enemy in proximity. It involves a series of defensive and offensive moves designed to eliminate the threat quickly. The goal is clear: **take the enemy out before he takes you out.**

But in marriage, using that approach against each other only leads to wounds. When you fight *against* your spouse, you damage the very person you're meant to protect. Many marriages suffer from emotional, mental, and even physical wounds that were never meant to be inflicted. Strife, resentment, and division create self-inflicted wounds, making it easier for the enemy to move in and attack at our weakest moments. Instead of **fighting against each other**, you must **fight hand-in-hand together.**

This means:
- Holding onto your spouse in tough times instead of pushing them away.

- Recognizing that your spouse is not your enemy but your strongest ally.
- Protecting each other from external threats instead of creating internal wounds.
- Choosing to fight for your marriage, not just in it.

The moments when my wife and I were apart the most—especially during my military service—were the moments when we were tested the hardest. There were times when we outright failed those tests, and we experienced firsthand how distance, silence, and lack of communication opens doors for the enemy to attack. But those experiences also taught us the power of fighting together instead of against each other.

If you're currently married, take a moment to reflect on how you're choosing to fight:
- Are we fighting each other or fighting together?
- Are we building our marriage or tearing it down with words and actions?
- Are we aligned in purpose or letting petty disagreements drive us apart?

If you're not careful, your marriage can become a **war zone** rather than a **place of refuge.** Remember that your **marriage is worth fighting for—but only if you're fighting the right fight.** When a husband and wife unite in prayer, purpose, and love, the enemy doesn't stand a chance.

The main point to take away from all of this: Unity in marriage doesn't happen by accident, it's *built, protected,* and *fought for.* When you stand together—hand in hand—you build something the enemy *can't* tear down.

Whew! That was a lot of groundwork! But with the foundation set, it's time to start building this house! In any structure, **beams** are crucial. They hold everything together, distribute weight, and keep the building stable.

Communication in marriage works the same way. Without it, even the strongest relationships can weaken and wither under weight. So, let's explore how solid communication can keep your marriage standing strong.

The Beams of Communication:

SPEAKING, LISTENING, AND RESOLVING CONFLICT

"The heart of the wise instructs his mouth [in wisdom]and adds persuasiveness to his lips." **Proverbs 16:23**

Communication is the Backbone of Marriage. In combat, clear communication isn't just helpful, it's a matter of life and death. On the battlefield, the ability to send and receive information accurately can be the difference between victory and disaster. Soldiers use coded messages, the phonetic alphabet (*Alpha, Bravo, Charlie*), or even Morse code to ensure they're understood, especially when the chaos of war makes miscommunication a costly mistake. Imagine sending an urgent message to your unit only to realize they never got it because you were on the wrong frequency.

Marriage works the same way.

If you and your spouse aren't communicating on the same frequency, even your best intentions can get lost in translation. Messages sent but not received lead to confusion, frustration, and division. And that's exactly what the enemy wants. If he can break communication between you and your spouse, he can sow seeds of misunderstanding, resentment, and emotional distance. Most disagreements don't stem from what was said...but from what wasn't clearly communicated or understood. When was the last time you and your spouse had a disagreement? Chances are, at the root of it was a breakdown in communication.

Maybe one of you felt unheard.

Maybe assumptions were made instead of questions being asked.

Maybe the timing was off, you know, that "We need to talk" moment *right before bed* or *as you're rushing out the door.*

Whatever the cause, here's the truth: **The strength of your marriage depends on how well you communicate.** So why do communication breakdowns happen in marriage?

Let's break it down:

- **Hearing isn't the same as listening:** Just because you heard the words doesn't mean you understood the message.

- **Assumptions fill in the blanks:** When we assume instead of asking, we often get it wrong.

- **Poor timing kills good conversations:** Even the right words can fall flat if delivered at the wrong moment.

- **Emotions cloud clarity:** Anger, frustration, or stress can turn a simple conversation into a full-blown argument.

The enemy thrives in these gaps...exploiting silence, twisting words, and magnifying offenses. When communication is **weak,** the entire marriage suffers. When it is **strong,** everything else can stand.

So, the question is: **Are the beams of communication in your marriage strong enough to hold the weight of life's challenges?** If not, let's lay the groundwork for healthy communication.

THE FOUNDATION OF EFFECTIVE COMMUNICATION

There are three key elements that make up strong beams of communication:

1. **Speaking with Intentionality**: Using words that *build, not break.*

2. **Listening with Understanding**: Hearing more than just the words your spouse says, it's about tuning in to their feelings, emotions, and what's really on their heart.

3. **Resolving Conflict with Wisdom**: Using healthy conflict vs unhealthy conflict

Let's break these down.

Speaking with Intentionality: Using Words That Build, Not Break

Words have **power.** They can build a bridge or burn it to the ground, sometimes in a matter of seconds. **Every word you speak in your marriage is either strengthening or weakening your bond.**

"Death and life are in the power of the tongue."
Proverbs 18:21

It's easy to let frustration drive your words, but intentional speech focuses on *connection,* not *correction.* Here are common communication pitfalls and how to avoid them:

a) **Pitfall: Speaking in Anger Instead of Truth**

- What it looks like: Lashing out when emotions are high.
- Solution: Use "I" statements to express feelings instead of "You" accusations.
- Example: "I feel hurt when I'm interrupted" instead of "You never listen!"

b) **Pitfall: Silent Treatment & Stonewalling**

- *What it looks like:* Shutting down instead of addressing the issue.

- **Solution:** When emotions run high, agree to revisit the conversation later.
- *Tip:* Say, "I need a breather. Can we talk in an hour?" instead of walking away in anger.

c) **Pitfall: Unclear Expectations**

- *What it looks like:* Expecting your spouse to read your mind.
- **Solution:** Clearly express your needs and desires.

Example: "I'd appreciate help with dinner this week," instead of hoping they'll notice you're overwhelmed.

Healthy communication isn't about being **the loudest or the most "right."** It's about fostering understanding and connection and speaking with **grace, wisdom, and patience.**

Tips for Intentional Speaking

- **Pause Before Speaking:** Instead of reacting impulsively, take a deep breath and consider how your words will land.
- **Choose Your Words Carefully:** Ask yourself, *"Will this help or hurt our connection?"*
- **Be Clear & Direct:** Avoid **passive-aggressive statements** or vague hints. Say what you mean with love.

A strong marriage requires both spouses to commit to intentional, kind, and honest communication.

Listening with Understanding:

Hearing Beyond the Words

Most people *hear* to **respond,** not to **understand.** But in marriage, true *listening* means tuning in to your spouse's *heart,* **not just their words.**

How to Become a Better Listener

- **Give Your Full Attention**: Put down your phone, turn off distractions, and *be present.*

- **Listen Without Interrupting**: Let your spouse express themselves before responding.

- **Validate Feelings Before Offering Solutions**: Sometimes, your spouse just needs to be heard, not "fixed." Try saying, "That sounds really frustrating, I hear you."

- **Ask Clarifying Questions**: If something isn't clear, ask: *"Can you help me understand what you meant when you said…?"*

- **Repeat Back What You Heard**: *"So what I hear you saying is…"* Ensures that you're on the same page.

When both you and your spouse **feel heard and understood,** disagreements turn into **conversations,** and conversations build connection.

Resolving Conflict with Wisdom:
Healthy Conflict vs Unhealthy Conflict

Conflict is inevitable in marriage, but how you handle it determines whether it builds *bridges* or *barriers*. Let's break down what healthy versus unhealthy conflict looks like:

Unhealthy Conflict Looks Like:

- Blaming and name-calling
- Yelling and shutting down
- Holding onto grudges

Healthy Conflict Looks Like:

- Seeking to understand
- Taking responsibility
- Finding solutions together.

Here are four steps you can take to resolve conflict in a healthy way.

Step 1: Pause & Pray Before Reacting

- *When tensions rise, take a breath. Ask yourself, "Is this worth damaging our connection?"*

Step 2: Define the Real Issue

- Are you arguing about the dishes...or feeling unappreciated? Dig deeper. Surface issues often mask deeper feelings.

Step 3: Focus on Solutions, Not Blame

- Shift the conversation from "What went wrong?" to "How can we fix this together?"

Step 4: Forgive & Move Forward

- Resentment poisons your marriage. Forgiveness clears the air so healing can begin.

Remember, the strongest marriages aren't built by accident. They are built through intentional communication. So let your words build, not break. Let your listening connect, not divide. And let your conflict resolution bring healing, not harm. Because when the beams of communication are strong, your marriage can withstand any storm.

Still, even the best communication needs *support*. Think of communication as the beams of your house. Without sturdy pillars to hold them up, even the strongest beams can collapse. Just as a house relies on sturdy pillars to bear weight and provide stability, your marriage needs strong pillars to reinforce your partnership. These pillars are trust, **support, and a shared vision.**

- ○ **Trust:** Provides security and emotional safety.

- ○ **Support:** Strengthens your bond through all seasons.

- ○ **Shared Vision:** Ensures you're building *together*, not apart.

Without these essential pillars, communication can buckle under life's burdens. But with trust, support, and a united vision, you'll not only *survive*, but you'll also *thrive*. Ready to explore how trust, support, and shared vision fortify that connection? Let's dive into the pillars that will help your marriage stand strong through every storm.

Pillars that Strengthen Your Partnership

TRUST, SUPPORT, SHARED VISION

THE PILLAR OF TRUST: HAVING EACH OTHER'S SIX

In combat, a soldier's survival depends on one crucial truth: **your battle buddy has your six.** That means they are covering your blind spots, protecting you from unseen threats, and standing guard when you're most vulnerable. This same principle applies to marriage: **trust is the pillar that assures both you and your spouse are truly safe with each other.** But trust in marriage goes beyond just physical protection; it is the foundation of **emotional, mental, and spiritual security.** Without it, uncertainty and doubt creep in, weakening your bond. Do You Feel Safe Enough to Be Vulnerable with your spouse? One of the greatest indicators of trust in marriage is the ability to be **fully seen, known, and loved** without fear.

Let's be honest, most couples in marriage struggle with being vulnerable. We certainly did. Real trust means you can expose your **fears, failures, and dreams** without worrying that your spouse will use them against you.

It means knowing that:

- Your spouse won't belittle your struggles.
- They won't **dismiss** your emotions.
- They won't **betray** your confidence.

Many people struggle with vulnerability in marriage because of past wounds. Maybe trust was broken in this relationship, a past relationship, or even in childhood. But marriage requires a level of trust that says, **"I see you completely, and I am still here."** Vulnerability isn't just about sharing your struggles, it's about believing your spouse will handle them with care.

I (Tacondra) remember the first time I had an anxiety attack in front of Eric while we were working together as claims adjusters. The job was overwhelming, and although I had more experience than him in adjusting claims, I was terrified to let him see me struggle. Up until that moment, Eric had never witnessed me in my element professionally, and I didn't want him to see me fall apart. But this time, I couldn't hold it together. I wanted to quit. Mentally, physically, and emotionally, I was at my limit. As I tried to explain what I was feeling, tears started falling, and before I knew it, I was in full breakdown mode.

Eric stood there, frozen—eyes wide, unsure how to respond. He wasn't used to seeing me like this. I had always been the strong one, the one who pushed through. But in that moment, I wasn't strong...I was raw, overwhelmed, and afraid of being judged for not having it all together. Would he dismiss my emotions? Would he see me differently? That moment wasn't just about the job, it was about trust. Can your spouse count on you? When life gets overwhelming, do they feel like they are facing battles alone, or do they know you have their back? Trust isn't just about words; it's built through consistency, presence, and the ability to hold space for each other's struggles, without judgment.

Being reliable in marriage means: Showing up, even when it's inconvenient.

Following through on what you say you'll do. Being emotionally present, not just physically present. And creating a safe space for open and honest conversations. You don't build trust in a day, but you can damage it in a moment. That's why even the small, everyday choices like being honest, keeping promises, and standing by each other are vital in reinforcing this pillar.

Assume the Best, Not the Worst

In the military, assuming the worst about your battle buddy can be dangerous. You operate under the belief that they are on your side, and that trust allows you to function as a unit. Yet, in marriage, couples often default to assuming the worst about their spouse's intentions. If they forgot something important, was it an attack, or just an oversight? If they reacted differently than expected, was it rejection, or just miscommunication? If they expressed frustration, was it aimed at you, or were they just overwhelmed?

When you start assuming the best about your spouse and seek to understand their heart rather than jumping to conclusions, you create a culture of trust instead of suspicion. Trust is not something you set once and forget, it's a daily commitment to be trustworthy and to extend trust. Just as a soldier depends on their battle buddy for survival, your marriage depends on knowing that you and your spouse have each other's six...always.

THE PILLAR OF SUPPORT: CARRYING EACH OTHER'S BURDENS

Another unshakeable principle in the military that guides every mission is: **no soldier is left behind.** When one struggles, whether from exhaustion, injury, or the weight of battle, the team doesn't move forward without them. Instead, they step in, lift them up, and carry what they cannot. Yep! You got it, marriage operates the same way! There will be seasons when one of you is weaker emotionally, physically, mentally, or spiritually. Life has a way of throwing curveballs when you least expect it. **The true strength of your marriage isn't revealed during the easy seasons but in how you show up for each other when things get hard**; even when those challenges aren't directly happening to you as a couple.

I (Tacondra) want to share a personal story that brought this truth home for us. On December 19, 2021, Eric returned home from a six-month civilian deployment in South Korea. We were ready to reconnect and enjoy the holidays together. But just three days later, right before Christmas, my father had a massive stroke. I've always seen myself as a warrior, resilient and strong, but nothing could have prepared me (or my family) for that day or the journey that followed.

While my mom, sisters, and I threw ourselves into caregiving, **Eric took a backseat to being nurtured in our marriage**, yet he never complained. He never made me feel guilty or like I was failing as a wife; not for the missed breakfasts, lunches, or dinners, not for unintentionally neglecting his needs due to exhaustion, and not even for the times I couldn't give him my full attention. I vividly remember asking him at one point, *"Why don't you just leave me?"* Because, truthfully, I felt like I was losing myself and him while drowning in a sea of grief from losing a version of my daddy that no longer existed. In the months that followed, other life storms rolled in. Any of which could have easily driven us apart. **But instead of pulling away, he leaned in.**

Eric jumped in the trenches with me, offering unwavering support caring for my father, all while navigating the heavy emotions life threw our way and carrying the financial responsibilities of our home. **That's the kind of love that holds you up when you feel like sinking.** It was during this season of our marriage that the vow *"in sickness and in health"* was truly put to the test. But what happens when *"in sickness and in health"* doesn't just apply to you or your spouse, but to your family members? Do you have the kind of love that sticks through those times? Or will you back away when the burden feels too heavy? Marriage is about carrying one another's burdens, especially when it matters most. It's easy to stand together when life is smooth, but the real test comes when the weight of hardship threatens to pull one of you down. Or the both of you apart. **In those moments, you have a choice:** step in and help carry the load or stand back, letting your spouse struggle alone out of selfishness and lack of capacity to honor your vows.

Marriage wasn't designed to be a solo mission. If one spouse is carrying the full weight of responsibility while the other is disengaged, resentment, frustration, and exhaustion will eventually set in. Support means sharing the load, recognizing when your spouse is overwhelmed, and stepping in to help before they collapse under the weight of it all. If your spouse is struggling emotionally, do you offer a listening ear or dismiss their feelings? If your spouse is physically exhausted, do you step in to ease their load, or do you expect them to push through? When they're spiritually drained, do you lift them up with prayer and encouragement, or leave them to navigate it on their own? Many men and women find praying over their spouse challenging. It can feel intimidating, especially if you're unsure how to pray or underestimate the power it holds to create intimacy in marriage, as we mentioned earlier in the pages of this book. *You become more intimate with whom you pray for, pray with and pray to.* We will go deeper into the details of intimacy soon. But here's the simple truth we want you to focus on now: **even a simple, whispered prayer is better than no prayer at all.** It's not about saying the "perfect" words, it's about inviting God into your marriage and covering your spouse with love and support. A few sincere words like, *"God, strengthen my spouse today and give them peace,"* can make a world of difference.

Do You See Their Struggles as an Inconvenience or an Opportunity to Love Them Deeper

It's easy to love when your spouse is strong, independent, and meeting your needs. But what about when they are struggling? When they are not themselves, not as affectionate, or not as engaged as usual? **True support means loving your spouse even when:** They are dealing with stress and anxiety. They are facing personal disappointments or failures. They are physically unwell or exhausted. They don't have the strength to pour into you like they usually do. Are you prepared for the seasons that will come to teach you that love isn't just about feeling connected in the good times, it's about standing firm in the hard times? Now please don't hear what we are not saying. **Remember this:** support isn't about waiting for your spouse to always be strong; it's about stepping in and being strong for them when they can't be.

So, how can you better serve and uplift each other in everyday life? The strongest marriages, as we've explained, don't rely on grand gestures but on small, daily choices to serve and uplift each other.

Let's review some simple but powerful ways to show support:

1. Check in with your spouse daily…ask how they are really doing.

2. Step in before they ask for help…if they're stressed, take something off their plate.

3. Be their safe space…create an atmosphere where they can share their burdens without fear of judgment.

4. Pray for them and with them…spiritual support is just as important as emotional and physical support.

5. Encourage them often…sometimes, just hearing *"I see you, I appreciate you, and I'm here for you"* makes all the difference.

Unity Means Walking Through Battles Side by Side

Let's lighten things up for a moment as we continue diving into the power of unity. Marriage isn't about keeping score over who's carrying more weight, it's about recognizing each other's strengths and walking through life's battles together without blame or resentment.

In our marriage, I take on the role of provider, protector, and leader, making sure our home stays stable and secure. Tacondra, on the other hand, is the visionary. She's the dreamer and sees the bigger picture with bold ideas and foresight that keep us moving toward our purpose. Now, some might say the man should be the visionary, but in our case, she's the one with the telescope, and I'm the guy holding the map, figuring out how to get there. Thanks to my military background, I'm a task-driven man, which has helped us view this balance as a strength, not a struggle in our home. My wife being a visionary doesn't mean I lack vision, it means I have a clearer lens because I have her help. It took us years to fully understand and appreciate this dynamic, but now we see how well it works for us.

The truth is, there will be seasons when you carry more and others when your spouse does. But it's never about who's holding the heavier load, it's about making sure neither of you carry it alone. A true partnership is about lifting each other up, filling in the gaps, and moving forward as one team. At the end of the day, it comes down to this simple truth: when things get heavy, you don't let go, you hold on tighter.

THE PILLAR OF SHARED VISION: FIGHTING FOR THE SAME MISSION

In the military, a battle buddy isn't just there to watch your back, they're there to keep you focused on the mission. Without a clear objective, soldiers would wander aimlessly, wasting energy (and probably arguing over whose turn it is to navigate) while missing what really matters. Marriage works the same way. If you and your spouse aren't working toward a shared vision, you'll feel like you're pulling in opposite directions, like two people trying to steer the same boat with different maps.

Here's the thing: most couples don't struggle because they lack love. They struggle because they lack **clarity** on what they're building together. *Been there, done that!* We totally understand. Love gets you to the wedding, but **shared vision and direction** carry you through the marriage. As we mentioned earlier, every strong structure starts with a blueprint. So... have you and your spouse talked about what you're building? Or are you just reacting to whatever life throws your way? Like dodging bills, juggling kids, and arguing over what's for dinner (again)? Here are some big questions to consider:

- Are we intentionally creating a life together, or just surviving day to day?
- Is our marriage reflecting love, unity, and purpose, or just routine?
- Are we working toward peace in our home, financial stability, personal growth, and leaving a legacy?

If you don't define what you're building, distractions and disagreements will define it for you. And trust us, *Netflix binges and endless to-do lists* won't get you closer to your goals. *Although, we must admit, Netflix binges are fun and create time for intimacy!* A shared vision keeps your marriage anchored, even when storms come.

WHERE DO YOU SEE YOUR MARRIAGE IN FIVE, TEN, TWENTY YEARS

A soldier in battle isn't just thinking about the next step, they're thinking about the mission's end goal. Likewise, marriage isn't just about surviving through the week; it's about thriving through the years. Every strong marriage needs vision. Without a shared direction, you can drift into routine, frustration, or even misalignment. In our Built2Last Marriage Bootcamp we encourage couples to create a **marriage mission** that serves as a compass and keeps you grounded in why you're together and where you're going. It gives purpose to your partnership and helps you navigate seasons of struggle and seasons of growth when you feel tempted to give up. Just like businesses thrive with a mission statement, marriages do too. It's not about perfection, it's about intentionality. When you take the time to sit down, seek God together, and write a mission for your marriage, you're declaring: **This is what we stand for. This is what we're building. This is what we're committed to becoming together.**

Take time together to answer these questions:

- What kind of marriage do we want five, ten, or twenty years from now?
- How do we want to grow spiritually, emotionally, and financially?
- What legacy do we want to leave behind for our children and future generations?

Dreaming is great, but planning is what turns dreams into reality. Prioritize your goals and make daily choices that move you closer to them.

MARRIAGE MISSION TEMPLATE

Our Marriage Mission Statement

(Write this together, guided by prayer and honest conversation)

We, _____ and _____, commit to building a marriage that is rooted in _____, guided by _____, and fueled by _____.

Our purpose together is to _____.

We choose to honor, protect, and grow with one another through _____. In our home, we will value _____, prioritize _____, and cultivate _____.

Together, we will serve _____, build legacy through _____, and glorify God by _____.

Signed:

_____ (Husband)

_____ (Wife)

Date: _____

Aligning Your Individual Goals with Your Shared Purpose

Before you said, "I do," you were two individuals with different dreams, gifts, and callings. Marriage isn't about losing yourself, it's about aligning your strengths for a shared purpose. As mentioned before, in our marriage, we've discovered a rhythm:

Tacondra is the visionary; she dreams boldly and imagines what's possible. I'm the strategist; I focus on how to make those visions a reality, step by step. Instead of arguing over who should lead, we've learned to embrace how our differences complement each other. It's not about competition; it's about collaboration.

Ask yourselves:

-How do our gifts and skills complement each other?

-How can we support each other's personal callings while keeping our marriage first?

- What adjustments do we need to make to stay aligned on purpose? When you align as a team, your differences become your greatest asset.

A United Marriage Has Direction. When a marriage has a clear mission, everything else will likely fall into place. Even when circumstances change—jobs shift, seasons transition, or unexpected hardships arise—your commitment to each other and your shared vision will remain firm. So, the question isn't just where are you going individually? The question is where are you going together? Because when you and your spouse fight for the same mission, there is no battle you cannot win.

TAKEAWAY CHALLENGE:

This week, look your spouse in the eyes and say: *"We're on the same team."* Then:

- Ask how you can better support their goals.
- Dream together about your future.
- Celebrate the small wins along the way.

Hold on tighter when things get heavy, because the best teams never quit on each other. Marriage is a partnership, it's endurance, and standing together through every season. While both husband and wife make sacrifices, **some sacrifices go unseen, unspoken, and often unacknowledged.** This is especially true for my wife and other military spouses, who silently shoulder the weight of long separations, unpredictable changes, and the constant demand to adapt.

Tacondra will take a moment to share these **hidden sacrifices of a military wife: the emotional battles, the quiet strength, and the resilience it takes to hold everything together while their partner serves.** Because sometimes, fighting for your marriage isn't just about what happens when you're together, it's about how you hold on, even when miles apart.

Silent Sacrifices: The Unseen Journey of a Military Wife

Let me begin by saying that being a military spouse is an honor. Yet, it's an honor that often comes with hidden burdens, battles, and silent sacrifices that are rarely understood or fully acknowledged, both within and outside of the military community. Only a military wife can truly grasp what it means to be one, to carry the weight of both pride and pain in the same breath. Being a military wife means living in the background while your spouse wears the uniform upfront. It's understanding that "service" really extends beyond the one wearing the fatigues, and experiencing how it infiltrates every part of your life. For many military wives like myself, the biggest sacrifices aren't just the deployments or the relocations; they're the internal battles. The fight to maintain your identity, the exhaustion of surviving and maintaining the household alone, and the tension between being strong because you have to versus because you want to.

Supporting your spouse's career often requires putting your needs, dreams, and even your marriage dynamics on the back burner, and that can weigh heavily on your heart. As a veteran wife, I want to take time in this chapter to peel back the layers of what it means to be the woman behind the uniform. The one standing in the gap. Not just for your family but for your marriage, and how those silent sacrifices can either build a stronger foundation or slowly chip away at the commitment and connection you share with your spouse.

LOSING YOURSELF TO FIND YOURSELF

Marrying into the military isn't just a life choice; it's a lifestyle. Overnight, you become more than a wife…you're "the spouse." At first, you might embrace it, diving into volunteer roles and embracing the community to fit in. But for some, like me, that connection and community doesn't come easily. I struggled with finding my place back then, and honestly, it's something that still affects me today. Over time, you often learn how to be alone, even amid others. But at some point, along the line of adapting to this new life, you will catch your reflection in the mirror one day and wonder: "Who am I beyond this uniform that isn't even mine?" For most wives, especially those married young or during early adulthood like I was, your dreams—if you even had the chance to dream—often end up taking a backseat. You once envisioned a thriving career or hobbies that defined you, but plans shifted when you said, "I do". Nothing truly prepares a military wife for the quiet grief that comes with sacrificing her ambitions or putting them on hold, patiently waiting to discover her own dreams, all for the sake of her family's stability. Some spouses pursue their passions or explore different career paths while navigating the journey. However, these endeavors are often short-lived due to starting over with each PCS (Permanent Change of Station), unless they involve entrepreneurial pursuits that offer the flexibility military life demands. You might land a job you love, only to leave it two years later. Or you give up on applying for roles entirely because "Why bother? We'll be moving soon." The instability wears on you. New cities, new homes, new routines, and sometimes, the painful task of reintroducing yourself to people who will only be in your life for a season. Finding fulfillment often requires creativity, sometimes shifting from focusing on a "career" to doing something that feels meaningful and has purpose.

MOTHERHOOD, BEING STRONG, AND THE CHALLENGES OF LETTING GO:

Motherhood under normal circumstances is already challenging. Especially when you're a young mom and feel as if you're still a baby *with* a baby. But motherhood in the military is another battlefield altogether. You're often "the voice" that the children listen to mostly as the default parent. There are times you're the sole parent, attending parent-teacher conferences, comforting children missing their other parent, and explaining why Dad (or Mom) can't be there for the big recital or game. Your children may struggle with being in community due to the constant moves, leaving friends, changing schools, and adapting to new environments. You hold it together for them, wiping tears, encouraging resilience, and teaching them to embrace change. But deep down, you wrestle with guilt. *"Are they getting enough stability?"* *"Am I enough for them when I'm running on empty?"*

Supporting your spouse's career often means putting your needs aside to *be* the stability of the family. Most times you are the decision-maker, you become both the nurturer and protector, and the fixer of everything that breaks the moment they leave. You tell yourself, "I'm strong enough for this," even when tears stain your pillow at night. Love keeps you anchored, but it's not always easy when the distance grows longer, and the silence stretches wider.

Sometimes, resentment creeps in; not because you don't support them, but because you wonder when someone will support you. Who sees the hours you spend managing the household, navigating everyone's emotions, and fighting your own loneliness? Who acknowledges the times you paste a smile on your face, assuring everyone you're "fine" when you're carrying the responsibilities of two people? Becoming the strong one is as much a burden as it is a blessing, carrying weight that often goes unseen yet deeply felt. You quickly realize you don't get the luxury of falling apart when things get hard, and it seems like everything rests on your shoulders. Not because you wanted to carry it all, but because *there was no other choice.*

The kids get sick—*you're the one at the doctor's office.*
The car breaks down—*you handle it.*
The car catches a flat tire—*you have to call USAA*

The microwave breaks, roof leaks, bills pile up, school projects loom—*it's all you.*

You become strong out of necessity, not desire. And while this resilience can be empowering, it can also harden you. You learn to suppress vulnerability because there's no time or space for it. Tears are reserved for the shower, after the kids are asleep. You learn to muzzle complaints, especially when your spouse is dealing with their own battlefield stressors. But over time, that strength can morph into *independence that isolates.* You get so used to leading, deciding, and managing that letting your spouse back into those roles, if they ever occupied them, feels unnatural, even frustrating because you've been running the ship. You think to yourself, *"Why do I need help now?"* Or worse, *"Why should I trust you to lead when you never have because you're always gone?"*

CHALLENGES OF LETTING GO

Allowing our husbands to lead not only in our marriage but also in the home after prolonged absences is one of the most profound struggles military wives face. While the military thrives on structure and chain of command, family life doesn't always operate the same or as easily. When your spouse returns from deployments, there's often an expectation, both from them and from you, that they'll step back into their leadership role. But what happens when you've already filled that space for months or even years? What happens when you don't know how to let go and let him lead?

The tension is real:

- You develop a routine with the kids. Now Dad has opinions that disrupt what's been working.
- You manage the finances, make tough calls, and handle discipline and now letting go feels like surrendering control.
- Your spouse wants to "reclaim" his place, but you're thinking, *"Where was this involvement when I needed help?"*

Trust me, it's not about disrespect or a lack of love, it's about the survival mode you must adopt. And the impact of constantly living in survival mode weighs on you. Even after the active-duty rodeo is done. When you're forced to function as both parents, caretaker, and decision-maker, reverting to a co-leadership dynamic can feel like undoing months of hard-earned stability. On the flip side, your husband may feel displaced, like a guest in his own home. His intentions to lead are often met with resistance or a lack of competency, not because you don't value him or want him to lead, but because you're exhausted and protective of the systems you put in place to survive. This can create a cycle of frustration: he pulls away, you feel unsupported, and resentment builds on both sides.

These are the thoughts, emotions, pressures, and complexities a military wife navigates; often misunderstood or overlooked by others. So, how do you navigate this complex dance of independence and unity? How do you honor the strength you've built without diminishing your spouse's role as a leader? I wish I had known then what I know now. Some of these strategies I've learned and applied over the years as a veteran wife, while others are still a work in progress.

HERE ARE A FEW PRACTICAL STEPS YOU CAN TAKE:

1. **Communicate Expectations Before Homecomings:**
    Reintegration isn't just about physical return; it's
    about emotional and mental re-entry. Talk about
    what's working at home, what changes your spouse
    can ease into, and where you genuinely need help.

2. **Be Honest About Your Struggles:**
    Let your spouse know it's hard to hand over the reins,
    not because you don't trust them, but because you've
    carried so much. Vulnerability creates space for
    empathy.

3. **Create Space for His Leadership:**
    This is easier said than done but, start small. Let him
    handle certain decisions or routines. It's okay to guide
    but resist the urge to control every detail. And if he
    doesn't do things right at first, it's okay! Give him
    grace.

4. **Address Resentment Head-On:**
    Unspoken frustration lingers. If you're harboring
    bitterness over past absences or felt burdens, bring it
    to light lovingly. Healing begins with honesty.

5. **Celebrate the Team You Are:**
    Remember, marriage isn't about keeping score. It's

about recognizing that you're on the *same side.* You were strong when you had to be, and now, it's about sharing that strength together.

The beauty of navigating these challenges lies in the opportunity to *strengthen your foundation.* When you learn to endure seasons of forced independence and emerge committed to teamwork, your marriage eventually becomes stronger.

THE INVISIBLE BURDEN:

Lastly, the hardest part of being a military spouse is the silent nature of the sacrifices. There's no medal for holding the family together, no parade for the nights spent alone, no awards for the sacrifices you make behind closed doors. People thank your spouse for their service (and rightfully so), but they often overlook you. Living in the shadows as a military wife can even extend beyond the uniform, quietly affecting other areas of your life. Unaware, you often become the foundation upon which others build, carrying the weight of supporting their dreams and visions, often at the expense of your own. You nurture others' businesses, ideas, projects and goals, while your own dreams, strengths, gifts, goals, and visions often remain overlooked, underappreciated, uncultivated or incomplete.

And maybe you're not a military spouse, but this resonates deeply. You've supported your husband in ways no one else sees. Through silent seasons of sacrifice, through transition, through dreams deferred and strength sustained behind the scenes. Your story may not involve military deployments, but it may include separations, long hours, and the emotional toll of his occupation. And that carries the same weight of commitment and selflessness. You've been the steady anchor, the quiet intercessor, the unseen strength that holds everything together.

The truth is, you're a silent warrior. You carry the weight of many roles without applause. And though you didn't take an oath to wear the actual military uniform, you live the cost of service every single day.

But know this: I SEE YOU. You ARE a foundation. And *your sacrifice matters.* The love you pour into your family, the stability you create, the resilience you model, it's invaluable. You are the base and the balance that allows your spouse to serve with peace of mind, knowing home is taken care of. That's not small. That's monumental.

Being strong because you *have to be* is a reality I know all too well. But one important lesson I've learned throughout my journey is that strength isn't just in carrying the load, it's also in knowing when to lay it down. It's in allowing your spouse to step in, even when it feels easier to just keep doing things yourself. It's in choosing *partnership over pride.*

Marriage in the military isn't always fair, and it doesn't get easier after transitioning back to the civilian lifestyle. But with communication, grace, and a shared commitment to grow through the challenges, you can build a marriage that not only withstands the pressures of service and the life storms that ensue afterward, but flourishes despite them.

You are strong. You are resilient. And together, you're *unbreakable*.

Better together. Built to last.

The Dimensions of Intimacy: Mind, Body, Soul

Intimacy in marriage is something we all crave, yet it can also be what we fear the most. Why? Because true intimacy demands vulnerability—the kind that exposes your deepest thoughts, dreams, and insecurities. It's one thing to be loved; it's another to be fully known and still deeply cherished.

Many marriages don't suffer because spouses **stop loving each other,** but because they fail to truly **know each other.** There's a difference between *knowing* your spouse and *knowing of* your spouse. Knowing your spouse isn't just about being familiar with their habits or daily routine. It's about understanding their mind, connecting with their body beyond physical acts, and intertwining your spirits through shared purpose and faith.

Thriving intimacy is built on three interconnected layers: **mind, body, and spirit.** Neglect one, and the connection weakens; nurture them all, and your bond will flourish.

1. Intimacy of the Mind (Intellectual Connection)

True intellectual intimacy goes beyond surface-level conversations. It's about genuinely engaging with your spouse's thoughts, passions, and dreams. When you understand how they think and what excites or challenges them, you create a space where both of you feel valued and heard.

Now, take a moment and think about your own marriage. When was the last time you and your spouse had a conversation that lit you up on the inside? Not just about bills, kids, or schedules, but about purpose, dreams, or what's stirring in your hearts? Do you know what challenges your spouse mentally or inspires their creativity? Have you allowed yourself to be seen, not just emotionally or physically, but *intellectually?*

So many couples are surviving on surface-level exchanges, when their souls are craving deeper connection. Real intimacy doesn't start in the bedroom; it starts in the mind. It begins with curiosity, active listening, and being fully present with the one you vowed to grow with.

Before we dive into how to build intellectual intimacy, ask yourself this: "**Have I created a space where my spouse feels safe to think, dream, and be vulnerable with me?**" Because the truth is, when the mind is engaged, the heart, and even the body, often follows.

How to Build It:

- Ask thought-provoking questions about life, dreams, and goals.
- Explore books, ideas, or new experiences together.
- Be curious about your spouse's thoughts, fears, and aspirations.
- A strong intellectual connection creates strong **emotional security** and keeps curiosity alive in your marriage.

2. Intimacy of the Body (Physical Connection)

Many couples assume physical intimacy is just about sex, but it's much more than that. True physical intimacy begins with touch, affection, and affirmation long before it reaches the bedroom. Intimacy is cultivated in the small, everyday gestures that say, "I see you; I cherish you." It's in the intentional hug before walking out the door, the hand resting gently on their back during prayer, the playful flirtation while washing the dishes, cooking dinner, or folding laundry, and the forehead kiss after a hard day. These aren't just motions, they're ministry.

Genesis 4:1 says, "And Adam knew his wife, Eve." This wasn't just about a physical act; it represented oneness, deep connection, and belonging. That word "knew" speaks of intimacy that involves the whole person...mind, body, soul, and spirit. When physical intimacy is approached with that level of reverence and love, it becomes a beautiful expression of covenant, not just chemistry.

So, are you making room in your marriage for non-sexual touch and connection? Do you treat physical closeness as a sacred language of love, or as a task tied to expectations? Have you allowed busyness, exhaustion, or unspoken disappointments to rob you of affection that your spouse and your marriage deeply needs? If so, don't be discouraged. We've been there too. We've walked through seasons of physical drought in our marriage and times when connection felt distant and desire dimmed under the weight of life. But the one thing we've learned is this: **physical intimacy isn't just about what happens in the bedroom, but what happens before it and because of it.** It's not only about being desired, it's about being intentionally pursued.

Let's explore how to kindle or rekindle physical intimacy in a way that reflects love, honor, and sacred pursuit.

How to Deepen It

- **Show Daily affection**: Hugs, holding hands, kisses, and gentle touches
- **Physical attraction**: Compliment and appreciate your spouse's appearance and efforts.
- **Healthy sexual intimacy**: Prioritize a healthy sex, but remember, emotional closeness fuels physical connection.

Physical connection should never grow stagnant, it should deepen over time, just like the other dimensions of intimacy.

3. Intimacy of the Spirit (Spiritual Connection)

Spiritual intimacy is the deepest level of connection, and it starts not with your spouse, but with God. The spiritual aspect of our lives is often the most overlooked, especially if spirituality isn't something you focus on regularly. But whether or not you consider yourself spiritual, the truth remains: **you are a spirit, with a soul, living in a body**. Still unsure? Well... just try holding your breath indefinitely and see what happens. (You won't be here long!) Your spirit is the core of who you are. The part of you that connects to something greater than yourself. Ignoring it doesn't make it any less real; it just leaves an essential part of you neglected.

And trust us, we've been there. Tacondra has always been a passionate prayer warrior. She could go from calm to calling fire from heaven in 0.2 seconds. Meanwhile, I, Eric, (writing this in full transparency) used to feel completely inadequate when she asked me to pray. I'd think, *"Uhh... after all that? You want me to follow that up?"* My prayers felt like a soft whisper compared to her thunder! And Tacondra, with all love and good intentions in her heart, had unknowingly placed this expectation on me to be the "prayer leader" in a way that didn't fit how God was growing me.

Eventually, we realized we had to release each other from roles we were never meant to force. She's responsible for her relationship with God. I'm responsible for mine. But when we come together? It amplifies everything. Because you become more intimate with the one you pray for, pray with, and pray to. The closer you are to God, the closer you should become to your spouse. Just don't try to control or clone your spouse's spiritual journey, *God's got that covered.*

Let's explore ways to strengthen spiritual intimacy together.

How to Strengthen It:

- Pray Together: A marriage that prays together stays stronger.
- Read and Discuss Scripture: Let God's Word be a guiding force in your relationship. Not a weapon to rule, reign, or lord over your spouse with. That's being religious.
- Worship Together: Whether through song, devotion, or shared moments of gratitude.

- Encourage each other's faith journey without coercion or comparison.

You become more intimate with the one you pray for, pray with, and pray to! The closer you are to God, the closer you'll be to your spouse.

At its core, spiritual intimacy and prayer serve as a covering for your marriage. It's not just about growing closer to one another, it's about building a hedge of protection around your union. When you pray together, you invite God into the center of your covenant, and that divine alignment creates a shield from outside forces. Prayer keeps your hearts soft and your unity guarded. It helps you fight the real enemy, not each other, and reinforces the foundation of your faith when life's storms hit. Because storms will come. But couples who cover one another spiritually are better equipped to weather them. That's why prioritizing spiritual intimacy isn't optional, it's essential.

Now, let's talk about the roof and how to guard your marriage from external storms.

The Roof of Protection: Guarding your Marriage from External Storms

Every well-built home needs a covering. Its job? Protection. Roofs shield everything inside from rain, wind, heat, and those surprise storms that roll in out of nowhere. Without it, you're vulnerable to leaks, damage, and some seriously damaged and soggy furniture. Marriage is no different. Without protection, your relationship is like a house with no roof, exposed and at risk. Your marriage isn't just a good thing, it's a God thing. A covenant designed to flourish, grow, and withstand the test of time. But here's the reality: anything valuable will be tested. Storms will come in the form of distractions, outside influences, and spiritual attacks that threaten to weaken your union. The question is, are you guarding your marriage, or leaving it wide open?

Just like unpredictable weather, external storms in marriage don't always come with warning signs. Sometimes they hit hard and fast, other times they creep in quietly. Without intentional protection, outside influences can slowly erode the love and trust you've worked to build. Let's break down the most common "weather patterns" that can threaten your relationship and how to weatherproof your marriage.

THE STORM OF OUTSIDE OPINIONS — PROTECTING YOUR MARRIAGE FROM UNHEALTHY INFLUENCE

Ever noticed how everyone suddenly becomes a marriage expert with advice to give the minute you say, *"I do"*? Family, friends, coworkers? Some of it is helpful; a lot of it...not so much. It's easy to let those outside voices sneak in, but ask yourself: Are other people's opinions shaping how I see my spouse? Do I run to friends before communicating with my partner? Are family members overstepping boundaries in our relationship? Not every voice deserves a seat at your table. Wise counsel is valuable, but not every married couple is thriving, and not every well-meaning friend understands the depth of your commitment. The only voices that should truly shape your marriage are God's, yours, and your spouse's.

How to Guard Against This Storm:

- Set clear boundaries with family and friends. Your marriage comes first.

- Choose trusted mentors who value biblical marriage principles.
- Communicate with your spouse before seeking outside advice.

THE STORM OF COMPARISON— PROTECTING YOUR MARRIAGE FROM UNREALISTIC EXPECTATIONS

Social media, movies, and even other couples can make it seem like someone else's marriage is more exciting, more romantic, or more successful than yours. But what you see on the surface rarely reveals the full picture.

Comparison is like a slow leak in your marriage roof; it seems harmless until it floods your joy. What comparison steals:

- **Contentment:** You focus on what your marriage *lacks* instead of its *strengths*.
- **Realistic expectations:** You start measuring your spouse against highlight reels; an impossible standard.
- **Gratitude:** You overlook the good in what you have while longing for *"more."*

God gave you and your spouse a unique relationship; custom-built for your growth, purpose, and fulfillment. Always remember that what works for others may not be what God designed for you. And that's okay. Embrace contentment in your portion because you never know if what you're admiring in someone else's marriage is actually their hidden struggle.

How to Guard Against This Storm:

- Focus on your marriage. Celebrate small wins and daily joys.
- Practice gratitude. A thankful heart keeps resentment at bay.
- Limit social media scrolling: Your relationship deserves better than constant comparison.

THE STORM OF BUSYNESS AND NEGLECT — MAKING TIME FOR YOUR MARRIAGE

Life gets busy...we get it. Careers, kids, ministry, bills... it all adds up. Before you know it, "We'll talk later" turns into days, then weeks of barely connecting. And slowly, your marriage starts to feel more like a business partnership than the love story it was designed to be. Neglect doesn't come with sirens or flashing lights. It shows up quietly, one missed date night, one overlooked hug, one "I'm too tired" at a time.

For us, it showed up in the small ways we chose to unwind. Tacondra is a reader. She can get lost for hours in reading multiple books and not even realize the time. I enjoy watching TV. Give me a good series or game and I'm in the zone. We realized that if we weren't intentional, we'd end up spending our downtime apart, slowly drifting from one another without even noticing. So, we made a choice. Now, we *choose* to do more things together. Whether it's binge-watching a Netflix show we both enjoy, or me taking time to listen to her passionately explain key points in the newest book she bought (even if I still don't know what she's reading about!). It's not about changing each other, it's about choosing connection over convenience.

If you are married, where in your marriage have you unknowingly opened the door to disconnection? Are you living *together* but feeling worlds apart? Storms don't always come with thunder, they sometimes show up in silence. And if you're not careful, the storm of neglect can wear down the intimacy you've worked so hard to build.

How to Guard Against This Storm:

- Prioritize time together: Even short, meaningful conversations can reconnect you. Schedule *Netflix* nights! Yes, even if it's just watching your favorite show together.
- Check in regularly. Ask your spouse, *"How are we doing?" "How can I love you better?"*
- Don't let schedules dictate your intimacy. Love is an intentional choice, not just a feeling.

THE STORM OF TEMPTATIONS: STOPPING THE CANCER OF EMOTIONAL AND PHYSICAL AFFAIRS BEFORE IT SPREADS

Marriage is a beautiful union, but let's be honest, it's also a place where two imperfect people will, at some point, hurt each other. Especially if you marry young and must navigate the journey of growing up together. Making mistakes is inevitable, but willfully causing harm or having ill intent toward your spouse is Intentional, not accidental. Learn to distinguish the difference between the two so that love doesn't blind you from exiting out of a marriage designed to break you. Whether intentional or unintentional, offense is inevitable, but unforgiveness is optional. Holding onto past hurts is like carrying a backpack full of bricks; the weight doesn't just slow you down, it wears you out. We all want love that lasts but love without forgiveness is impossible. If you're in marriage long enough, you will have to forgive your spouse for something, big or small. Maybe it's words spoken in frustration, an unmet expectation, or a deep wound that cut to the core. Whatever it is, forgiveness is the glue that holds a marriage together when everything else tries to pull it apart.

With that being said, prepare yourself for this conversation; especially if it hits home in your marriage. Talking about the dreaded emotional affairs and infidelity isn't easy, but it's necessary! No one wakes up one day and suddenly has cancer. The truth is that it starts silently, hidden beneath the surface, with abnormal cells multiplying before any symptoms appear. By the time it's detected, the disease has often been growing for months or even years. Infidelity in marriage, whether emotional or physical, works the same way. Infidelity doesn't begin in the bedroom; it begins in the heart and mind. Like cancerous cells that lie dormant before multiplying, emotional entanglements often start with small compromises. At first, it's barely noticeable: a casual conversation, a lingering glance, a craving for attention. But if left unchecked, it spreads like a malignancy, weakening trust, attacking intimacy, and threatening the life of the marriage.

We wish we could say our marriage was immune to this, but we weren't. I served three year-long tours overseas, and while the physical distance was tough, it was the emotional distance that proved more dangerous. I often found myself in conversations with women struggling in their own relationships. I thought I was just being a listening ear, offering harmless support. But their need to be heard met my need to feel needed. By the time I realized I was giving attention away from my wife, the emotional connections had already formed. Tacondra, on the other hand, felt the shift at home. When trust began leaking from our marriage, resentment quickly filled the gaps. She held onto the hurt, refusing to forgive. That bitterness made her vulnerable, and soon, attention she wasn't receiving from me found her. Her heart, already in a broken condition at the time, had opened to outside validation. That alone gave the enemy enough room to further divide us.

We learned the hard way: unhealed wounds will always feed themselves if you don't surrender your hurts to God. Emotional infidelity doesn't come crashing in, it creeps in through cracks left unattended. And what you feed... grows.

At first, it seems insignificant, just like a single cancerous cell. But **what you feed grows.** Like a slow-growing tumor, emotional entanglements metastasize, growing deeper, demanding more attention, and ultimately leading to full-blown betrayal. We wish we could say our marriage was immune to this, but we weren't. Like many couples, we didn't see the disease forming at first. By the time we recognized it, the emotional damage was already spreading.

How Infidelity Cancer Spreads*

If You Don't Catch the Disease of Infidelity, It Spreads
Like an untreated cancer, **infidelity progresses through different stages:**

Stage 1 – Exposure (*Initial Cell Mutation*)

- You form a connection with someone outside your marriage.
- You begin talking **more openly and honestly** with them than with your spouse.
- You **downplay the interaction** because "nothing physical" has happened.

Stage 2 – Justification (*Tumor Growth Begins*)

- You convince yourself it's **harmless** (*"They just listen better"*).
- You **start comparing** your spouse to the other person.
- You become **more distant** in your marriage without realizing why.

Stage 3 – Full-Blown Emotional Affair (*Cancer Spreads to Other Areas*)

- You **crave** their attention and feel excitement when they reach out.
- You **hide messages, delete conversations,** or sneak away for calls.
- You start **minimizing your spouse's value** in your mind.

Stage 4 – Physical Infidelity (Terminal Stage – Marriage at Risk)

- The emotional bond turns physical.
- You're **fully invested in deception,** believing you're too deep to turn back.
- The disease has now **metastasized**—causing deep wounds in your marriage.

How to Guard Your Marriage from Infidelity:

1. Cut Off What Feeds Temptation

- If you don't want to eat the forbidden fruit, **stay away from the forbidden tree.**

- **Set strong boundaries:** Stay away from situations that make compromise easier.

- **Avoid private, overly personal conversations with the opposite sex.**

- **Be honest with yourself.** If you're looking forward to talking to someone a little too much, that's a red flag.

- **Rule of Thumb:** If your spouse wouldn't be comfortable with the connection, it's already crossed the line.

2. Treat Issues Early (Before They Spread)

Ignoring cracks in your relationship won't make them disappear. Like untreated cancer, they'll only grow.

- **Have honest conversations with your spouse.** *"Are we still fully present for each other?"*

- **Identify weak spots.** *"What needs aren't being met, and how can we fix it?"*

- **Heal past wounds.** Resentment left unchecked becomes a breeding ground for temptation.

3. Strengthen Your Marriage Immunity

Healthy marriages don't just happen, they are built daily.

- **Be intentional about intimacy.** Don't let your relationship run on empty.
- **Pray together.** Spiritual connection creates protection against temptation.
- **Invest in each other.** What you nurture at home, you won't need to seek elsewhere.

Early intervention makes all the difference. Healing is possible, but it starts with honesty, accountability, and God's grace. Storms are inevitable. Distractions will come. Temptations will arise. But when your marriage is covered with **intentional protection**, you'll stand strong even when the winds howl, and the rain pours. Guard your heart. Guard your time. **Guard your GOOD (and GOD) thing.** No fleeting temptation is worth a lifetime of regret.

Bombs on the Battlefield: Recognizing the Unseen Attacks on Your Marriage

Marriage can feel like a battlefield. The enemy knows he can't always launch an outright attack on your relationship, so instead, he aims to wear you down through something we call **battle fatigue**. Those subtle, exhausting hits that chip away at your connection over time. These attacks don't always come as obvious explosions; sometimes, they sneak in like hidden landmines buried beneath the surface, waiting for just the right moment to detonate. Ever felt stuck in a cycle of stress, distant silence, or the same argument on repeat? That's the battlefield in action. The good news? You don't have to stay defenseless. It's time to expose the enemy's tactics and take back your ground. We're going to break down **the five biggest bombs** planted in marriage:

Battle Fatigue, Complacency, Cycles, The Pressure to Provide, and Family Struggles, and inform you how to disarm them before they destroy what you've built.

Battle Fatigue

Battle fatigue is real. It creeps in when couples feel like they're fighting the *same battles* over and over again. It's that exhaustion that sets in after months—or years—of trying to hold everything together. You're giving it your best, but eventually, the weight of marriage, responsibilities, and life starts to feel like a backpack full of bricks.

Symptoms of Battle Fatigue in Marriage:

- Feeling stuck in repetitive conflicts: *"Didn't we just have this argument last week?"*
- Carrying the pressure to provide without relief.
- Juggling family, kids, work, and responsibilities with no time to recharge.

Why is this dangerous? Because when you're exhausted, you're vulnerable. The enemy doesn't need a dramatic attack; a **small temptation, subtle lie, or misplaced frustration** is enough to cause cracks in your relationship.

How to Disarm It:

- Understand that rest isn't a weakness, it's a weapon. Running on empty isn't heroic. Prioritize rest and recharge. Your marriage deserves the *best* of you, not what's left of you.

- Recognize the warning signs: If you and your spouse are constantly drained, irritable, or disconnected, it's time to evaluate what's causing the fatigue.

- Make space for joy: Everything doesn't have to be so serious! Laugh together, be silly, and remember what drew you to each other in the first place. Sometimes a spontaneous dance party in the kitchen (or in a public setting outdoors) can do wonders.

Complacency: When Comfort Becomes a Trap

Complacency is sneaky. Unlike a sudden explosion, it *slowly* erodes connection over time. It's like a soldier who stops wearing his helmet because "*nothing has happened yet.*" One of the many lessons you would learn if you went to war is that complacency is your number one enemy. Why? Because it puts yourself and everyone around you at risk. Something leaders in the military would constantly say to us when I served was, "Keep your head on a swivel!" Translation? Stay alert—danger doesn't take a day off. The number one cause for soldiers to become complacent on the battlefield is battle fatigue. The same goes for marriage. This happens in marriage when you get exhausted from the mundane of doing the same things day in and day out. You take each other for granted because *"they'll always be there."* **Prioritizing convenience over communication because:** *"It's not a big deal... they'll get over it."* Before you know it, what used to be special becomes *meh*. Conversations shift from deep talks to quick logistics: *"Did you pay the bill?"* or *"Who's picking up the kids?"* And romance? *Yeah... what's that again?* When these things happen, you become vulnerable to the enemy's attacks.

If you haven't fallen victim to this yet, we are sure you will at some point because it's inevitable. Our advice is not to get overly confident and comfortable in your marriage and ignore the signs that you or your spouse are getting complacent or fatigued. Stay alert—don't let routine replace romance. Keep your head on a swivel! Do not brush things off that are slightly off kilter about you or your spouse's behavior just because you don't want to deal with small foxes that may arise. **Call out the drift.** If things feel "off," say so. Ignoring small shifts creates bigger gaps later. **Create new experiences.** Routines aren't bad, but it is exciting to try something new together. Perhaps, something different like randomly moving out of the country to Belize for three months! *Yep, we did that.* Remember, your spouse and union deserve your focus, attention, and intention.

CYCLES: BREAKING FREE FROM REPEATED PATTERNS

Ah, the dreaded cycles. That feeling of constantly going around the frustrating rat wheel of the same arguments, issues, and frustrations. Ever thought: *"Didn't we just deal with this last week, last month, or last year?"*

"Why does this keep happening?"
"I feel like we're stuck on repeat."

Yep, us too. *Been there, argued that.* And after a while, the whirlwind of confusion and frustration leads to full-on battle fatigue. Marriage comes with seasons and habits, but when the same negative patterns keep showing up, it's not just a season, it's a *cycle*. And cycles don't break themselves.

We've lived through this in more ways than we can count; spiritually, emotionally, mentally, and especially financially. It felt like no matter how far we thought we had progressed, we'd somehow find ourselves right back at square one. *Cue Brian McKnight's "Back at One" music playing in the background.* But trust us, it wasn't romantic, it was *frustrating.*

There was even a particular season where we were struggling financially and spiritually, and it felt eerily similar to one we had experienced five years earlier. That was the wake-up call. Tacondra kept calling out the patterns and finally got my attention. We had to face the truth: it wasn't just bad luck or another rough patch. It was me. Her. *Us.*

Our behaviors, habits, and unaddressed issues were keeping us on that cycle. There were lessons we didn't fully learn the first time, and God, being the loving Father He is, wasn't going to let us skip the process, again.

Seasons will change on their own. But cycles only change when you do. If you don't identify the root of the pattern, you'll just keep dressing it up in different seasons. Growth requires us to address the root issues, not just in our marriage, but in *ourselves.*

How This Bomb Works:

- Unhealed wounds create repeated triggers.
- Patterns from childhood, past relationships, or previous hurts shape reactions.
- Little offenses get swept under the rug… until the rug explodes.

How To Disarm It:

- **Get to the root:** Stop treating surface symptoms and start identifying what's really causing the cycle.
- **Commit to change:** If you keep doing the same thing, you'll keep getting the same results. Be intentional about breaking the pattern.
- **Pray for wisdom:** Some patterns are spiritual battles. Invite God into the cycle-breaking process. His guidance can bring clarity you didn't know you needed.

THE PRESSURE TO PROVIDE: CARRYING THE WEIGHT OF RESPONSIBILITY

One of the heaviest burdens in marriage, especially for husbands, is the **pressure to provide.** But let's be honest, wives feel it too. Whether it's providing financially, emotionally, or spiritually, carrying the weight of responsibility can become overwhelming. Many of us, regardless of gender, silently battle thoughts like: *"I can't afford to fail,"* or *"If I drop the ball, everything falls apart."*

Let's rewind to the beginning: When God created Adam, He placed him in the garden with clear instructions—to **cultivate, nurture, and steward** what God had given him. Adam's first roles were naming the animals and tending to the garden, highlighting his responsibility and authority. It wasn't until after Adam's work had begun that God introduced Eve, forming the first marriage covenant, a partnership designed for unity and shared purpose. Interestingly, Adam did not feel the burden of "providing" in the way we understand it today. In the garden, every need was met. Provision was God's responsibility, and Adam's role was stewardship. But when sin entered the picture, everything changed. Adam now had to *toil* for survival; a reminder of how disconnection from God's provision leads to striving and stress. Fast forward to modern times, and society has layered on even more pressure. Society often teaches men that their worth is tied to their earnings or how well they provide. Women, too, face the expectation to juggle it all: career, family, home, and emotional support. The result? A generation of husbands and wives **carrying invisible weights**, afraid to admit how heavy it's become.

God did not stop providing, but He allowed man to feel the weight of his sin. Perhaps, to remind us that we still need God's help. Many young boys grow up being told their primary responsibility is to work, earn money, and provide shelter and food for their families. While these are important duties, this incomplete way of thinking places an immense amount of pressure on men, making them believe that their **sole purpose in life** is to provide materially. We often look at the order of creation—Adam first, then Eve—and assume that this makes women less significant. But order **does not diminish significance; it provides clarity and purpose.**

Work is ingrained in a man's nature, but it should not define him or limit his ability to contribute beyond finances such as: being emotionally present and engaged with their spouse and children. This silent struggle leads to battle fatigue, a weariness that cannot be relieved by sleep alone. The burden of always holding everything together becomes exhausting, and the sweat from our brows feels like blood dripping down our faces.

What we often fail to do is rest—not just physically, but in the finished work of Christ. Yes, Adam failed, but Jesus rose. When we learn to depend on and trust God as our ultimate provider, we can step back into our original calling—not just to work and toil, but to cultivate, nurture, and steward what God has already provided. True provision does not come from endless striving, but from aligning ourselves with God's divine order. **Where there is God's provision, there is no pressure to provide.**

HOW THIS BOMB WORKS:

- **Work replaces connection:** The focus shifts to providing instead of being present.
- **Pressure turns into burnout:** One spouse feels exhausted, while the other feels neglected.

- **God's provision is forgotten:** The burden feels like it's all on you instead of trusting Him.

How To Disarm It:

- **Remember, God is the ultimate provider:** You're not meant to carry it all alone.
- **Communicate about stress:** Don't suffer in silence. Share the load with your spouse.
- **Make space for rest:** Even Jesus rested. Taking a break doesn't mean you're failing, it means you're wise.

The Pressure To Produce: From A Woman's Perspective

From a woman's perspective, the **pressure to produce** can feel just as heavy, though it often wears a different mask. From the moment we say, *"I do,"* many of us feel expected to be nurturers, supporters, and problem-solvers. Society often tells us that our worth is measured by how much we *do* and *give*. We hold families together, anticipate needs before they're spoken, and juggle invisible loads all while trying to keep it together. And while we may not always be the ones out in the workforce earning a paycheck, we are always producing—producing love, stability, wisdom, and the unseen, invaluable contributions. If we're not careful, the constant pouring out leads to burnout and **resentment**.

But just like men need to rest in God's provision, **we need to rest in His grace.** Our value isn't in how much we produce, it's in who we are in Him. When we surrender the weight of expectations, we find peace in *being* rather than constantly *doing*.

How This Bomb Works:

- **Unrealistic Expectations:** The woman feels forced to constantly perform—whether as a wife, mother, career woman, or homemaker, often feeling that failure in one area means failure in all.

- **Emotional & Mental Overload:** Carrying the invisible load of remembering, planning, and anticipating the needs of the household while also maintaining personal goals and responsibilities.

- **Neglecting Self-Care:** Consistently prioritizing others' needs over personal well-being, leading to burnout, resentment, exhaustion, and eventually feeling invisible.

How to Disarm It:

- **Speak up about your needs:** Let your spouse know when you feel overwhelmed instead of silently sitting with it.

- **Set healthy boundaries:** Learn to say **no** to unnecessary demands that drain you and **yes** to things that restore you.

- **Prioritize rest & self-care**: Rest is not a reward for hard work, it's a necessity. Take that nap. Go for that walk. You matter.

- Share the Load: Don't carry everything alone. Ask for help and allow others, including your spouse, to support you.

- **Make Space for Joy** – *Being* is just as important as *doing*. Dance in the kitchen. Laugh until you cry and make room for fun in your marriage.

FAMILY: BALANCING MARRIAGE AND EXTERNAL RELATIONSHIPS

Remember those early dating days? Late-night conversations, spontaneous adventures, and *all the attention on each other*. Then...family dynamics entered the chat. Suddenly, you're balancing in-laws, traditions, and helpful advice like, *"When are you having kids?"* Family is a blessing, but it can also bring demands, division, and unexpected tension. While marriage is meant to bring peace and unity, it is not a band-aid for deeper issues. If left unaddressed, family pressures can drain the energy and connection out of your relationship.

The good news? **You have permission to protect your marriage**. Genesis 2:24 says:

"A man leaves his father and mother and is joined to his wife, and the two become one flesh"

We call this the **"leave and cleave"** effect and it is not just a suggestion, it's a necessity. A strong marriage requires healthy boundaries with extended family so that you and your spouse can build your own foundation.

Then comes another layer of change…children. While children are a gift, whether they came before or after marriage, they also shift the dynamic. It's easy to prioritize parenting over partnership, but here's a truth bomb: The best thing you can do for your children is invest in your marriage. One day, the kids will leave, but your spouse will still be there. Trust us, we know! Make sure you still *know* each other when that day comes. Make time for each other now. Keep dating, schedule getaways, and don't lose sight of the bond you share outside of parenting. **Your children are watching and learning not just from what you say, but from how you love.**

HOW THIS BOMB WORKS:

- Extended family oversteps boundaries, causing division.
- Parenting takes priority over the marriage, leaving spouses disconnected.
- Unresolved family baggage from childhood affects how you show up in your marriage.

How to Disarm It:

- Set healthy boundaries. Family should support your marriage, not interfere with it.
- Prioritize your spouse. Your kids are important, but your marriage is the foundation of your home.
- Communicate as a team. Make decisions together, and don't let outside opinions divide you.

The added strain of the areas we just discussed goes to show just how much we must contend with and fight for in marriage. Life consistently demands energy and effort, inevitably causing fatigue. The key is not to ignore it but to learn how to combat exhaustion with intentional rest and a sustainable pace that leads to success. Take a moment to evaluate the areas in your life and marriage that are most depleted. Where do you need renewal? Identify it and give yourself permission to rest in that area. Call a timeout, take a step back, ask for help—whatever it takes to restore yourself and your marriage, do it.

PHASE 3

RESTORING WHAT'S BEEN BROKEN

BECAUSE EVEN THE BEST-BUILT HOUSES FACE DAMAGE

Restoring What's Been Broken in Your Marriage

We intentionally waited to share more about this part of our story until now because it perfectly illustrates the importance of a strong foundation, not just in homes, but in marriage. Remember, in the beginning we told you about us building our first home. As new homeowners, we were overjoyed by this accomplishment. Everything about it was intentional. We handpicked the interior features, customized certain aspects to make it uniquely ours, and even chose the perfect lot. One with no homes behind us, giving us a sense of space and security. We even took a step of faith before the foundation was poured. Standing on that bare dirt, we wrote out a prayer on a piece of paper and buried it beneath where the front door would stand. It felt symbolic. Brick by brick, we watched our dream take shape. Every visit to the construction site made the reality of homeownership more exciting. **Everything looked perfect...until it wasn't.**

Within the first three years, we started noticing subtle but concerning issues. Yes, houses naturally settle over time, but what we experienced went beyond normal wear and tear. Cracks formed in the walls, doors wouldn't close properly, bricks began shifting and cracking, and the very foundation we trusted to hold our home was failing. Our house was literally standing on a prayer! Turns out, the soil beneath our home was never fit for building. For ten years, we lived in that house, navigating the emotional rollercoaster of dealing with a weak foundation. Eventually, after a draining two-year legal battle with the builders, we made the difficult decision to sell the home we'd built and walk away. It was painful. It was disappointing.

But it taught us a lesson we'll never forget: **No matter how beautiful something looks on the outside, if the foundation is faulty, it will eventually sink.**

Let's get real. Does This Sound Like Your Marriage?

Does your marriage *look perfect* **from the outside—photos, date nights, happy moments—but feel like it's cracking beneath the surface?**

Maybe the foundation was rushed, skipping important steps. Maybe past wounds, unresolved issues, or unspoken expectations were buried instead of addressed. Maybe time and adversity revealed weaknesses that no one saw at first. The truth is, most marriages don't fail because of one big issue, but because of small, neglected issues that weaken the structure over time. Like hairline cracks that seem harmless... until the wall caves in.

Our experience as homeowners mirrors the reality of many marriages. What starts as a dream, full of excitement and promise, can eventually reveal hidden flaws that threaten its stability. Every married couple starts with a vision of a perfect marriage; an expectation of love, security, and strength that will carry them through life's storms. But as time passes and reality sets in, you realize that your marriage, much like a house, requires maintenance, repairs, and sometimes even major renovations.

Just as homeowners are responsible for regularly maintaining their homes and taking precautions to prevent damage, you have the same responsibility in your marriage. To nurture, protect, and strengthen it against potential cracks and storms.

Both of us are licensed property and casualty home adjusters. We've seen homeowners invest everything into their houses, only to watch storms, floods, and fires wreak havoc. Some homes had obvious destruction; damaged roofs, collapsed walls, shattered windows. But others had hidden damage; cracks in the foundation, slow leaks causing rot, unseen structural weaknesses that threatened the home's stability before the storm ever occurred. Usually, when homeowners file claims after a storm, many of them focus on **what they can see.** The missing shingles, the water stains on the ceiling, the broken fences. But as adjusters, we are trained to recognize that the most dangerous damage is often unseen.

Marriage is no different. Some wounds are visible, others stay hidden beneath the surface, slowly weakening the foundation of your relationship. When conflict arises, trust is broken, or old wounds resurface, it's easy to focus on what's visible: the arguments, the distance, the frustration. But what about the unseen damage?

- The silent resentment that builds from unresolved issues.
- The emotional walls put up after trust is broken.
- The small cracks in communication that widen over time.

Ignoring these issues doesn't make them disappear. Patching over them without addressing the root cause only guarantees that you are delaying disaster.

THE CRACKS ARE A WARNING SIGN, NOT THE END

Homeowners often feel defeated when they see cracks in their walls or notice the roof is leaking again, despite previous repairs. Some feel like they wasted their time fixing things that didn't stay fixed. The same can happen in marriage. How many times have you thought: *"We already dealt with this issue! Why is it coming back?" "No matter what we do, something else always seems to go wrong." "Maybe this is beyond repair."* But here's the truth we learned from dealing with a faulty foundation in our own house and in restoring homes and helping people rebuild:

Cracks don't mean your house is beyond repair, they mean it needs a deeper level of restoration.

The real challenge is not whether damage will happen in your marriage, but how you choose to restore what's broken. One of Tacondra's well-known sayings is, **"The promise of restoration sounds good, but the process of it doesn't always feel good."** Restoring a marriage is like rebuilding a home the right way. Real restoration is tedious, messy, and requires tearing down weak areas before rebuilding them stronger. No matter how damaged your marriage may feel—whether from past trauma, childhood wounds, broken trust, or new pain that arises— it is worth restoring. Why? Because **Godly marriage was never designed to be disposable.** Mark 10:9 reminds us:

"What God has joined together, let no man put asunder."

And here's something we often forget: **"No man" includes us, too.** We don't want to be the main reason our own marriage falls apart.

Just as we learned from our experience as home adjusters, true restoration requires five key steps:

1. Choosing Renovation Over Replacement

One of the biggest temptations for homeowners facing severe damage is walking away from the house altogether. They assume it would be easier to start over with a new home than to put in the work to restore the one they have. Likewise, in marriage, when the damage feels overwhelming, the idea of walking away can seem like the best solution. Maybe you feel exhausted from the constant repairs. Maybe you're tired of dealing with the same issues. Maybe you wonder if something "new" would be easier than fixing what's broken. But here's what we learned in the field: **Replacing something doesn't guarantee you won't face problems again.** A brand-new house can still suffer storm damage, just like a new relationship will still face struggles. Instead of looking for something new, learn how to reinforce what you've built.

2. Assess the Damage Honestly

Before anything could be done to fix our home, inspectors had to fully evaluate the extent of the damage. It wasn't enough to fix what we could see—we had to identify the hidden weaknesses.

In marriage, **real healing starts with honesty.** You and your spouse must be willing to assess where the real problems are, not just what's visible.

3. Clear Out What's Broken

To properly rebuild a house, you must first remove the damaged areas. This is the hardest part of restoration; tearing down what's already damaged so it doesn't cause further harm. The same is true in marriage. Some things must be removed for restoration to take place:

- **Unforgiveness** – Holding onto past hurts will only deepen the cracks.

- **Pride** – Restoration requires humility, admitting where things went wrong.
- **Old Habits** – What worked in the past may not work now. Growth requires change.

Let's take a moment to dive deeper into the power of forgiveness, because it is the foundation for restoration.

THE POWER OF FORGIVENESS: THE FOUNDATION OF HEALING AND RESTORATION

Marriage is a beautiful union, but let's be honest, it's also a place where two imperfect people will, at some point, hurt each other. Whether intentional or unintentional, offense is inevitable, but unforgiveness is optional. Holding onto past hurts is like carrying a backpack full of bricks. The weight doesn't just slow you down, it wears you out. We all want love that lasts, but love without forgiveness is impossible. If you're in marriage long enough, you will have to forgive your spouse for something; big or small. Maybe its words spoken in frustration, an unmet expectation, or a deep wound that cuts to the core like infidelity. Whatever it is, forgiveness is the glue that holds a marriage together when everything else tries to pull it apart. Before we go deeper, let's make one thing clear: Forgiveness is essential, but staying in a harmful, toxic, or abusive marriage is not. If you are in a marriage where your spouse is intentionally harming you physically, emotionally, or psychologically, this is not a call to tolerate or justify staying in an unsafe situation. Love can be blinding, and many people stay in unhealthy relationships, mistakenly believing that enduring constant mistreatment is part of their commitment, often under the guise of religious obedience or misinterpretation of biblical teachings. That is NOT okay, OKAY?!

Forgiveness **is** for your healing, whether you choose to stay or walk away. It frees you from bitterness, but it does not mean staying in a cycle of abuse or justifying ill intent. If harm is being done, seek help, wise counsel, and safety. God's design for marriage is never for one spouse to be harmed, manipulated, or broken beyond repair. Now, with that said, let's talk about what true forgiveness looks like.

Many people struggle with forgiveness because they misunderstand what it really means. So, let's talk about what forgiveness is not:

- **Forgiveness doesn't mean forgetting...** at least not right away: It's possible to forget. But some hurts leave scars, and scars remind us of healing, not just pain. Forgetting is possible when you give the offenses over to God and let Him place them into the sea of forgetfulness. (Micah 7:19).

- **Forgiveness isn't approval**: It doesn't mean what happened was okay. It means you're choosing to release it, so it doesn't keep holding you hostage.
- **Forgiveness doesn't mean instant trust: We rebuild trust over time, but forgiveness is a choice we make in a moment.**

Forgiveness is not a feeling, it's a decision. And it's one that benefits you just as much (if not more) than it does your spouse. There are moments in marriage when forgiving feels impossible. When the wound is deep, the betrayal is painful, or the disappointment is heavy, it's tempting to cling to resentment instead of releasing it.

I (Tacondra) remember a time in our marriage when I wrestled with unforgiveness. I had been hurt, and even though I knew I needed to let it go, I wanted Eric to feel the weight of it first. Sound familiar? The truth is, unforgiveness doesn't punish your spouse, it punishes you. It keeps you trapped in a cycle of hurt, replaying the offense over and over in your mind. Eric, on the other hand, has always been quicker to forgive. Maybe because he felt like he'd caused more offenses in our marriage, or maybe not. Either way, I'll be honest, it used to frustrate me at times. But over the years, I've learned that **his willingness to forgive quickly wasn't weakness, it was wisdom.** He understood that holding onto offense only gave the enemy a foothold in our marriage.

WHY FORGIVENESS IS A SUPERPOWER IN MARRIAGE

Forgiveness in marriage is like renovating a house after a storm. If you refuse to fix the damage, the cracks will grow, the structure will weaken, and over time, the house will collapse. But if you take the time to **repair what's broken**, your marriage comes out stronger than before.

Here's why forgiveness is so powerful:

- **It breaks the cycle of hurt.** Without forgiveness, hurt people just keep hurting each other.
- **It restores emotional intimacy.** Resentment builds walls; forgiveness tears them down.
- **It protects your marriage from bitterness.** Unforgiveness allows small issues to fester into major divisions.
- **It models Christ's love.** If we expect God to forgive us, how can we refuse to forgive the one we vowed to love?

Colossians 3:13 (NLT) says, *"Make allowance for each other's faults, and forgive anyone who offends you. Remember, the Lord forgave you, so you must forgive others."*

That's a tough verse when you're hurting, but it's also a reminder that we've all needed grace at some point. If you're struggling with bitterness in your marriage due to unforgiveness, it won't stay hidden. It will show. It will show in the way you:

1. Speak to your spouse: Your tone becomes sharper, your words carry a sting, even in casual conversations. Instead of speaking with love and grace, your responses might be short, sarcastic, or laced with passive aggression. Resentment has a way of making even minor disagreements feel like full-blown battles.

2. Speak about your spouse to other: Maybe you vent to a friend, a family member, or even just replay the frustration in your own mind, highlighting all the things they've done wrong while overlooking any effort they've made to make things right. You might start focusing more on their flaws than their strengths, seeing them through **the lens of hurt instead of love.**

Unforgiveness has a way of hardening hearts and draining intimacy in a marriage. It builds emotional walls, creating distance where connection should be. If left unchecked, that bitterness doesn't just affect your relationship, it seeps into every part of your life, robbing you of joy and peace. The truth is, you can't love fully while holding onto resentment. Choosing forgiveness doesn't mean ignoring your pain, it means releasing it, so it doesn't control you. The way you speak to and about your spouse reflects what's going on in your heart. If your words are filled with frustration and bitterness, check what is fueling them. Ask yourself: *Is holding onto this hurt worth more than the peace we could have? Do I want to stay stuck in the past, or move forward together? What kind of marriage do I want to build? One filled with walls, or one built on grace?*

If you don't know HOW to forgive, here are the steps you can take:

1. Choose Forgiveness Daily. Forgiveness isn't a one-time event; it's a daily decision to release offense. Start NOW.

2. Communicate the Hurt: Don't bottle up your feelings, talk through them. But do it with love, not hostility.

3. Let Go of the Need for Revenge: Wanting your spouse to "pay" only prolongs your pain.

4. Set Healthy Boundaries: Forgiveness doesn't mean tolerating unhealthy patterns, it means working toward change.

5. Pray About It: Sometimes, forgiveness takes supernatural strength. Ask God to help you see your spouse through His eyes.

We're sure you've heard the old saying, *"holding onto resentment is like drinking poison and expecting the other person to suffer."* It's true.

Unforgiveness keeps you stuck, angry, and emotionally distant. But forgiveness? Forgiveness frees you. It lightens the load, brings healing, and allows love to flourish again. So today, make that choice. Not because your spouse always deserves it, but because your marriage does.

4. Rebuild with Stronger Materials

As home adjusters, we learned that proper materials are necessary to reinforce a foundation against future storms. A marriage built on lust, **temporary excitement, or external validation** will not last. But a marriage built on **God's principles, trust, and mutual commitment** will endure. Just like a house needs strong materials to withstand storms, rebuilding your marriage needs a stronger foundation to survive and thrive through seasons of difficulty. A weakly built house falls apart when pressure is applied. A well-rebuilt marriage stands firm because of the effort and materials put into it. So, choose carefully how you decide to rebuild.

If your marriage collapsed because you discovered it was built on **secrecy, selfishness, and neglect**, it's time that you rebuild it on **love, respect, and faithfulness.** Build with **Intentional Communication**. Not just talking but listening and understanding.

- **Trust & Loyalty**: Making integrity a priority, even in small things.
- **Grace & Patience**: Knowing that real growth takes time and effort.
- **Faith & Prayer**: Keeping **God as the foundation, not just a last resort.**

5. Maintain & Protect What You've Built

When we moved into our house, we assumed the foundation was solid. We didn't know it had hidden flaws. But now, with everything we've learned, we understand that even the best-built homes require regular maintenance.

Marriage is the same way. You don't just fix things once and assume they'll stay strong forever. You must continuously protect, nurture, and reinforce your relationship. You must **check in regularly.** Don't wait until there's a crisis to ask, *"How are we doing?" Prioritize connection.* Date nights, deep conversations, laughter…these keep the relationship alive. **Stay accountable.** Have people in your life who will encourage and support your marriage. **Pray together.** A marriage rooted in God's presence can withstand any storm.

Every broken marriage has the potential for restoration. But again, **restoration is not about just fixing what's broken, it's about rebuilding something even stronger.** If you believe God ordained and honored your marriage, then it is worth reinforcing, repairing, and rebuilding because once fully restored, it will stand strong through any storm.

PHASE 4:

MAKE YOUR HOUSE A HOME

A House Is Just a Structure, Home Is What You Create Inside of It

Making Your House A Home

Every house, no matter how well-built, is just a structure until life is breathed into it. The walls, foundation, and roof may provide shelter, but what truly makes it a home is what happens inside...the love, the laughter, the lessons, and the legacy you create. Think about your marriage in the same way. You've built your relationship, laid the foundation, strengthened the walls, and reinforced it against storms. Now, it's time to make sure it doesn't just stand, but it thrives. A house without furniture feels empty and cold, no matter how structurally sound it is. The same goes for your marriage. The relationship can survive on duty and commitment alone, but it thrives when it's filled with love, laughter, adventure, and romance. Think back to when you first got married. What did you love doing together? What made you laugh uncontrollably? What made you excited to see each other?

Now ask yourself: **Are you still doing those things?**

As time passes, it's easy to fall into routine, focusing on responsibilities and forgetting the joy of simply being together. But marriage isn't just about paying bills, raising kids, and making it through another day, it's about enjoying each other. Your marriage should feel like home, a place of comfort, safety, and joy. Make sure it's furnished with memories, not just responsibilities. A well-built home isn't just for those who live in it today, it's for the generations that follow. Whether or not you have children, remember that **your marriage is leaving a legacy.** The way you love, communicate, and treat each other teaches those around you (your children, family, friends, and even your community) what marriage is supposed to look like. Think about the marriages you saw growing up. Did they shape how you view love and commitment? Did they inspire you, or did they make you fearful of marriage? What do you want your children (or those watching your marriage) to learn from you? Because they are watching what you're building or what you're breaking.

Lastly, every home has a light that keeps it warm and inviting. Whether it's a porch light guiding you home at night or a cozy lamp that makes a room feel welcoming, light symbolizes connection, love, and warmth. In marriage, keeping the light on means choosing to nurture your relationship every single day because love isn't just a feeling, it's a daily choice. Even on the hardest days, when you're tired, frustrated, or busy, you have the choice to show up, to be kind, to communicate, and to love intentionally.

At the end of this building (or rebuilding) journey, we hope you remember this: A house is just a structure, it's what you put inside that makes it a home. Your marriage is the same. The foundation is commitment. The walls are trust, communication, and faith. The roof is protection from life's storms. And what fills it? Love, laughter, patience, grace, and memories that make it truly feel like home. So, what kind of home are you building? If you ever find yourself needing to rebuild or restore what life's storms have damaged in your marriage, remember that it is possible! And when it seems impossible, call on the **ultimate Master Builder**. The One who specializes in restoration and makes all things new:

JESUS CHRIST!

We pray that this becomes your commitment: **To not just have a marriage that lasts, but a marriage that thrives because it's anchored in unity, resilience, joy, intention, and love. You were made For Love, By LOVE.** And at the end of the day, you're better together! And with the right blueprint, your marriage will become Built2Last.

Build Well.

PRAYER FOR STRENGTH AND COMMITMENT IN MARRIAGE

Heavenly Father,

We come before You with grateful hearts, acknowledging that marriage is a sacred covenant designed by You. Thank You for the gift of companionship, love, and unity. As we commit ourselves to the vows we have spoken, we ask for Your grace to uphold them with integrity and faithfulness.

Teach us to love selflessly, to serve one another with humility, and to forgive as You have forgiven us. In times of abundance, may we remain grateful; in times of lack, may we remain steadfast. When trials arise, strengthen our bond and remind us of the promises we made before You.

Lord, help us to be patient, kind, and understanding toward one another. Guard our hearts against selfishness, bitterness, and pride. Let our marriage reflect Christ's love for the church, a love that is unconditional, sacrificial, and everlasting. We surrender our union to You, trusting that You will guide us through every season. May our love story bring glory to Your name and serve as a testimony of Your faithfulness.

In Jesus' name, Amen.

www.ingramcontent.com/pod-product-compliance
Lightning Source LLC
Chambersburg PA
CBHW071739120626

46550CB00002B/577